PARENTING

IN THE

REAL WORLD

The rules have changed.

Drop the guilt.

Handle any parenting situation in 7 simple steps.

BY STEPHANIE O'LEARY, PSY.D.

This book is meant to provide individuals with information, education, and support. It is
not designed to render professional advice or services to the individual reader. This book
is not intended to be a substitute or alternative for advice provided by a trained counselor,
therapist, medical doctor, or other similar professional. If you require such advice or
expert assistance, you should seek the services of a competent professional in the
appropriate specialty.

Message to Readers

This book is interactive! I am thrilled to show you how to bring it to life. All the QR (Quick Response) codes throughout the book can be scanned with your Smartphone or iPad to watch the videos that were created especially for you.

HOW TO SCAN THE QR CODES IN THIS BOOK

Step 1: Download a free QR code reader onto your smartphone by searching the App Store (I selected the Kaywa Reader because it is free of advertisements).

Step 2: Tap the app once it has downloaded to your phone; this will open up the Reader. Tap again, and your camera will appear to be on. Hover over the code you wish to scan, and the camera will automatically take a picture of the QR code; then your phone will be directed to the web page that contains each video message.

Here are some FREE tools

Grab "5 Simple Tips to Get Your Child to Listen."
http://bit.ly/2fnRprd

Be the first to know about Dr. Stephanie's latest Parenting Webinars:
http://bit.ly/2eNc4Bw

Keep up with the newest Parenting News:
www.StephanieOLeary.com

Join Dr. Stephanie on Facebook:
https://www.facebook.com/CPintheRW/

To Quentin, because there is no one else in the whole wide world I'd rather be doing this with.

Contents

Introduction

PARENTING IN THE REAL WORLD

Have you ever found yourself staring up at the ceiling in the midst of a chaotic family moment thinking, "This is not the kind of parent I want to be," but you have no idea how to change? Do you yell more than you want to, or feel like you're stuck in a repeating loop of dysfunction? Do you feel like it's too late to undo what's going on between you and your child and maybe even have some guilt about choices you've made up until now? Maybe you're getting by when it comes to parenting, or even feel like you have things under control, but want to simplify and optimize your approach. If you can relate to any of these perspectives, and if you appreciate that your chance to have a positive influence on your child is fleeting because time moves fast and old patterns repeat themselves—then *Parenting in the Real World* is for you.

Parenting in the Real World offers a roadmap to rediscover joy in parenting, a way to not only love your child but to really like him or her even if things are way off course. This comes in handy since you spend a ton of time together! These chapters offer a safety net, a wake up call, and a support system. We are all in this parenting game together and I want everyone—parents and kids—to thrive. It's never too early to start, but it's never too late to begin using this approach with your child.

Parenting in the Real World is different from other books you'll find because it leaves out all the fluff and focuses on basic strategies that will not only shift your parenting in a positive direction, but also build a foundation of trust, respect, and love so your child will want to spend time with you for years to come. The parenting skills in these chapters will help you navigate the daily grind while preparing your child for the real world. The changes you make will open lines of communication and allow your child to confidently deal with all of life's ups and downs now and in the future. There are certainly tools and quick fixes in these chapters that will amaze you the first time you use them, but the game-changing concepts I'm sharing will benefit you and your child for years to come.

The concepts you will find in these chapters are based on my years of training, clinical work, and personal parenting experience. I have worked with children for as long as I can remember—as a babysitter, a preschool teacher, and later as a caregiver for special needs children. While completing a five-year doctoral program in clinical psychology, I trained at Emory University Medical School's Autism Center where I learned volumes from expert supervisors and children who struggled profoundly, felt deeply, and often could not say a single word. My first official title was "family trainer," and I was continuously amazed at how impactful parenting tools were even in the most difficult of circumstances. I partnered to develop a program that allowed families from other geographic areas to access parenting support and continued to focus on the role of family dynamics and parent-child relationships as I earned my doctoral degree and specialized in clinical child neuropsychology.

As I assisted with cortical mapping procedures and tests to prepare children for brain surgeries, I developed a profound respect for brain-behavior relationships. This training cemented my belief that everything, every behavior, happens for a reason; that we—parents and children alike—are creatures of habit. Working hands-on with children who suffered traumatic brain injuries or intractable seizures that compromised specific neural regions taught me to never underestimate the role of biology, the resilience of a child's spirit, or the power of a parent's love.

As a post-doctoral fellow, I entered the clinical world by providing therapy services for children and families in a community mental health center in suburban New York. My skills were put to the test as I adapted research-based strategies to the unique and often complex circumstances of families from all walks of life. I learned early on that the best way to help a child is to help the child's parents—one session with a parent often accomplishes more than ten sessions with a child. I also learned that research is important, but any useful tool must be adapted to a family's real-world circumstances without judgment.

When I opened my private practice as a newly licensed psychologist my schedule filled quickly and I was not always able to accommodate new clients. At first I didn't understand why people would say, "But, it has to be you!" if I referred them to one of my highly qualified colleagues. I naively operated under the assumption that most people in my position shared my core beliefs and dedication to practical parenting strategies delivered without judgment. Now, almost a decade later, I understand that these principles set my practice apart. I am privileged to have supervised numerous clinicians seeking training in my approach and am dedicated to spreading the word and empowering parents. Most important, I have supported hundreds of families and continue to help clients move away from conflict and frustration while creating joyful, respectful homes.

In *Parenting in the Real World* you'll find seven straight-to-the-point, no-nonsense chapters that contain the game-changing tools I share with families every day in my practice. It's not rocket science. It's not super technical, or expensive, or even profound. Instead, these simple and practical parenting strategies will have a positive impact on your family right away, while setting the stage for positive parent-child interactions for years to come. Once you start practicing the steps outlined in these chapters you'll notice more listening and follow through, less conflict and drama.

I understand that creating amazing changes in your parent-child interactions is a tall order. I also know that parenting requires tremendous dedication and effort, so you only have time for strategies that work. The tools I share here are the same tools I use at home—and they truly make a difference.

I also know that parenting can be complicated, and I have experienced my fair share of not-so-glowing parenting moments over the years, including a few in the last week (OK, this morning). As a psychologist, I'm often approached by caregivers wishing to talk with me about their struggles. I listen, my wheels turning, as they share what goes

on in their homes, backseats, and backyards. I do my job diligently, looking

for patterns and offering suggestions to get things back on track. Amidst

the trouble-shooting and action planning, I really do get it because I have

been there too. I do not judge. Even when parents make quasi-confessions

about the words they say, the actions they take, and the things they think, I

have genuine compassion. Parenting is a hard job. At times, it can be

thankless with no vacation or sick days. You are on around the clock, and

that definitely creates a high-stress workplace.

The *Parenting in the Real World* approach takes all of the nitty-gritty

facts of life into consideration so you can be honest. Without honesty,

you'll wind up sweeping the ugly parenting stuff under the rug where it

never gets dealt with. It creeps out time and again, and all you can do is feel

guilty about it and then go right back to ignoring it. Rinse and repeat.

Clearly, that's not a very helpful loop. So I'm calling all aspects of parenting

out into the light of day. All the things I'm pretty sure happen in most

households that sap joy, rain on all the proverbial parades, and leave

parents and kids feeling crappy. That's the stuff I want to talk about—the

not-so-pretty, generally uncomfortable, real-world stuff. That is where you

have a genuine opportunity to create positive changes. I'll even share some of my very own parenting experiences, not because they are my proudest moments, but because it helps to know that we are all doing our best even when things are intense—or insane.

The other thing I want to point out is that I know what it's like to be on the front lines of parenting. I've been through a few of the phases so far, and have no illusions that the years to come will be clear sailing. I know what it is to worry, to have regret, to feel overwhelmed, and to be sleep deprived. I've been buried in laundry while desperately juggling the roles of wife, mother, neighbor, friend, and professional. I have teetered just on the verge of falling through the cracks only to look around see people who seem to have it all figured out. I know what it's like to judge myself, and I know that it gets me nowhere. I also appreciate that time goes by quickly, and there never seems to be enough of it to go around, so anything I devote my energy to must deliver results or it gets the boot.

The strategies you will learn in *Parenting in the Real World* take all of that into account. In these pages you will find simple, user-friendly parenting tools powerful enough to make a difference the first few times you use them. What you won't find is pages and pages of filler. These are the crib notes—the cheat sheets—so to speak. If you judge a parenting book by page count alone, I will probably disappoint you. If you value the content packed into each word, with room for a laugh here and there, then we're definitely on the same page.

In order for you to get the most out of *Parenting in the Real World*, I'll ask you to be as honest with yourself as I'm being with you. When you read these chapters, come as you are without judgment. It may be hard to face the messy stuff that's going on within your family, but if and when something hits a nerve or lands close to home, please power through it instead of shutting down or shying away. If some of the tools seem crazy, let them seem crazy and then give them a try anyway. You don't have a lot to lose. If you try the strategies and they don't work, you can go right back to doing things the way you have been. But maybe—just maybe—something will shift. Maybe you will see a reaction in your child or feel a change in yourself that is positive, even desirable. There is a chance that one of the seemingly simple ideas you read about can have a profound impact on your relationship with your child and on your quality of life as a parent. So, try it. You have so much to gain.

The other thing to know before diving into these chapters is that almost all of what I present has to do with changes you will be making. The net result for your family will still be what you want as a parent—kids who listen and get their points across respectfully and who are happy and generally compliant, right? I know this latter term is not necessarily the most popular, but let's air dirty secret number one here and now: all parents want their kids to comply—to listen. The tools I'm sharing will absolutely get you there, but they will also get you much further.

See, I don't want to create households where kids say, "yes, mommy" or "yes, daddy" and smile and do as they are told like puppets or robots. That's sort of creepy, and it's definitely not going to show up with any staying power here in the real world! Instead, my goal is to help your household be a place where kids and parents listen to each other and show respect for one another. Under these conditions, most of the time your kids will say yes when asked to do something, and as a bonus, they will also be happy more often than not. Plus, you will be able to tolerate them much more easily when they get upset—because here in the real world that's bound to happen. To bring things full circle here, this all culminates with parents feeling fairly happy too, and that's a fantastic end game. Win-win.

I'm going to help you reach big picture goals while tackling the day-to-day stuff you have to deal with no matter what. In the long term, I want your kids to want to hang out with you, to want to come home for Thanksgiving and birthdays even when they are all grown up and no longer have to. Working as a child psychologist for the past ten years or so has given me amazing perspective on the nature of parent-child relationships. I have the honor and privilege of hearing what children say about their parents and observing the way in which they try to make sense of the things they hear each day. I see kids learn to function in all sorts of family systems. Most families have good intentions, but even well-meaning parents sometimes create households that are not based on mutual respect and understanding. I get a front row ticket to the show that ensues, and it's not so great. Don't get me wrong, kids are incredibly resilient, and they generally do okay. However, I think we should aim for better than okay. I truly believe that kids and parents deserve to thrive, and that's why I'm making the time to share these thoughts with you and other parents who are motivated and looking for some practical guidance.

In *Parenting in the Real World* you will find tools to help raise children who believe they are worthwhile. The best way I can figure to help them buy into this idea is for them to go through life being treated with love and respect even when things are hard, even when you are tired, and even when they are not listening or respecting you in return. The tools and concepts presented in these chapters will help you navigate even the most difficult parenting calls with confidence. Confidence means less guilt; less guilt means more space for fun and joy. That's a great thing. You just have to pick a place to start and see for yourself how things unfold.

I do want to give you a bit of a road map before you start so you can chart the best course for your needs and your time constraints. There are seven chapters in this book, each devoted to a different topic and each filled with specific tools to help you start moving in a positive direction as soon as you're ready. Starting with chapters 1 and 2 probably makes the most sense because these chapters deal with the fundamental concepts of listening to, and validating (or truly hearing), your child. There is a lot of bang for your buck here because you can apply these tools and concepts to just about any situation, including the "in between times," also known as "regular life" when there is no crisis at hand. In fact, these tools and ideas may help you extend those regular times by heading off potential tantrums, conflicts, and standoffs. Plus, the information I share about listening and validating, as well as the tools that go along with them, are fantastic life skills. Practicing them with your kids will allow you to feel more connected and, in the end, when you listen, they listen, and everyone is happier. What more could you ask for, right? Your kids will be better listeners and will actually start to hear what you are saying to them. You may ask, "Is there really a need to read any further?"

Yes. However, feel free to skip around after Chapter 2. If a particular chapter appeals to you or seems especially relevant to your current situation, jump in. Here are the highlights.

Chapter 3 is all about how to communicate with your child respectfully. It's amazing how much impact your words have, and how small tweaks can make a huge difference in the way your message is received. If you find yourself saying the same thing over and over and only getting a response when you yell, scream, or slam something, check this chapter out. As you practice the tools discussed here, you will slowly start to see your children communicating with you, and with others, more respectfully. You do it; they follow (there is a method to this madness!).

Chapter 4 deals with setting limits—knowing when to say yes and how to say no, and to really mean both of them. There is also attention given to navigating negotiations and avoiding power struggles. If you find yourself constantly threatening to take away all privileges until there is no fun at all (i.e., canceling birthdays), or if you feel like a hopeless pushover who caves at the first sight of pushback, tears, or anger, this chapter is for you. This topic is one I hold near and dear to my heart because I see so many children struggling to cope with and accept boundaries and limits, especially now that we live in a society where instant gratification is prevalent. There's something for every parent in this chapter.

Chapter 5 is one of my personal favorites. It explains how to be accountable for your own actions. In short, this is all about learning to apologize to your kids and meaning it. Some people will breeze through this. Others may have a very hard time with the concept of saying sorry to a child, or to anyone for that matter. If you fall in this latter camp, please don't skip this one (and please fight any knee-jerk reaction to close this book right now). This is such a powerful tool. Not only will it help things move much more smoothly at home, but it will bring you worlds closer to your child. There is a lot to learn here.

Chapter 6 is about the art of rediscovering joy and falling in love with your child, possibly all over again. It's also about how to like your child amidst the day-to-day drama. This is the fun chapter, so I hope you don't need me to sell it to you. The strategies here will help you stop what you're doing in this busy, busy world and take time to appreciate who your child is as an individual. This chapter will help you gain some perspective after considering the big picture of parenting, and take a stroll down memory lane—as well as a glimpse into the future—by thinking about where your child will be in two, five, ten, and 20 years. This chapter will help you decide what you want your relationship with your child to be like as he or she grows and matures into an adult with all the freedom in the world. Spoiler alert, you may want to have a tissue nearby.

Chapter 7 is a chapter you may feel excited for or one you may be tempted to skip under the guise of "I've got that under control" or "I don't have time for that." It's all about the importance of self-care for parents. I see a lot of parents shy away from this and make excuses about the many reasons they cannot take care of their needs; however, self-care is a foundational concept of *Parenting in the Real World* because if you are depleted, exhausted, or unhealthy, there is no way you can use any of the tools in this book. Even if you read this chapter thinking it's total nonsense and not at all applicable to you or your home, please read it anyway. I would love for this to be the first chapter, but apparently that is not a very marketable position for it. So, please don't give up at the end. Your kids will thank you for taking this topic seriously, and self-care truly is fantastic once you warm up to it. Personally, I'm a fan.

Remember, start with Chapters 1 and 2. From there, dive in wherever you want to, based on your interests or needs. Remember too, no judgment. Go at your own pace, and see what makes sense to you. I figure, if there's even one thing you can relate to and apply at home, you're better off than you were when you started. It's all about trying to bring a little more joy to your parenting efforts.

CHAPTER 1

Listen:
The art of biting your tongue

Watch Video Message:
Dr. Stephanie O'Leary Introduces Chapter 1

http://www.stephanieoleary.com/intro-to-chapter-1-of-parenting-in-the-real-world.html

As a psychologist, I see children of all ages—and their parents—in my office. I also live with two children, a husband, an Australian shepherd, and a chocolate lab. The most common "complaint" I receive both at home and at work is that no one listens. Kids, mine included, routinely report that parents and siblings never listen to them, and that no one cares what they have to say. Similarly, parents, myself included from time to time, often feel that their children (and sometimes spouses, and frequently dogs) have an in-one-ear-and-out-the-other approach to communication. Parents do not feel heard either. Basically, according to the feedback I receive, households all over the place are virtual black holes of communication with lots of people saying lots of things and no one really hearing any of it. Sounds maddening, right?

I also know that this is a matter of perspective, and there are obviously times when the self-proclaimed unheard child is actually acknowledged and listened to. There are probably also many times when parents' suggestions (or pleas) are carried out by their offspring, mine included. I know that these things happen. Yet, many times, kids and parents still feel like no one is listening.

Let's face it; being heard is something we all desperately long for. When someone listens to us, we feel a connection. We feel that we are not alone. Being heard is inherently validating and it often sends us the message that what we have to say is important and worthwhile. We feel respected, on some level maybe even fulfilled. Sure, being listened to may not always be this glamorous and impactful. Sometimes, when we're just going through the paces of life, listening and being acknowledged allows things to flow a little more easily. But I'm sure you have been in the presence of a great listener at some point in your life, someone who has the ability to connect with you and genuinely hear you. If you're lucky, you have some great listeners in your inner circle. Being around them is easy because you feel they understand you, or at least put the effort in to pay attention to what you say and hear what's important to you. On the flip side, I'm sure you have been in a situation where you were not being listened to. You know, those exchanges where you find yourself repeating statements and possibly increasing your volume until you may even be shouting. In fact, this may have happened already, perhaps a half dozen times, today. This type of exchange feels frustrating. You wind up feeling like what you have to say is unimportant. If you are invested in your message, you probably wind up feeling confused and angry.

So, we have established that being listened to is much better than not being listened to. The good news is that this topic involves not doing much of anything (except listening). No major hoops to jump through and no complicated flow charts to follow. That means you get off easy, right? You sit back, relax, and listen away. Just to be safe though, let's take a look at the art of listening and review some things you can practice to make sure you are on the right track.

IN THE BEGINNING: LISTEN AND RESPOND

Parents are actually quite practiced at listening. When new parents are charged with the safekeeping of a tiny, helpless, fragile infant, they suddenly pay all sorts of attention to any cry, peep, or squeal that passes those adorable lips. It's a matter of survival, and some might say new

parents err on the side of hypervigilance. I myself was often accused of

borderline paranoia by my own mother who assured me that countless

generations of infants survived without the use of baby monitors or crib

pads that sounded an alarm if no motion was detected. Our modern

society definitely sends us the message that listening to our baby's every

sound and every move is crucial.

So, we do what good parents do. We listen and we respond. Baby

cries, we feed or burp or hold or change. Baby squeals, we look and smile

and laugh. And the cycle repeats. It's a great cycle, and it works out just

peachy for all involved. Side note, I know that I'm romanticizing a bit here

by leaving out the sleep deprivation and all the times when your best

responses don't seem to do a thing, but you get the point. Parents are

trained and conditioned early on to listen and respond. Those two actions

are fused together because they serve you, and your child, well. Listen and

respond becomes your autopilot.

Great, right? Something works, so score one for parents! Well, sure.

For a good long time the listen-and-respond marriage works out. Even

after your tiny, helpless, fragile infant starts toddling around and chatting

up a storm, you basically listen and respond and all is well. It works through the phase of endless questioning. Mommy, what is a platypus? Daddy, what are stars made of? Where were you? Where are we going? Are we there yet? Here, we listen to the question and we respond with an answer. The cycle usually continues, potentially ad nauseam, or until sleep sets in.

At a certain point though, the things our kids say to us start to change. There is an evolution in their communication as their sponge-like brains soak up more and more knowledge and information. At a certain point, they stop asking so many questions. And the ones they do ask are pretty practical. Can Jack come over today? When I finish my homework can I play on the computer before dinner? What time will you be home?

These are functional questions, not really teaching moments. Yet again, listen-and-respond, the virtual Batman & Robin of parenting communication, comes through for you. It's still totally appropriate. It will work here.

And by the way, when parents say, "No one is listening," this is what they are talking about. Parents know and love the practical listen-and-respond. They sort of expect their kids to start doing it as they grow up. I mean, we've been doing it throughout our entire parenting careers—is it too much to ask for a little reciprocation? Just answer me. Sometimes I don't really care if you do it or not, I would just like to know my words are not coming out in foreign tongues. I digress. This is what parents know and trust, and it is what they expect from their children.

However, when children say, "No one is listening," they are talking about something completely different. See, with age also comes more sharing. Not so much questioning to solicit information from you, but sharing about personal experiences and thoughts and even feelings. Young children do throw these sharing statements out there, but with maturation you will probably hear a lot more of what your child has to say. And when kids share, they do it with the expectation that you will really listen to them. They truly want to be heard.

Do you sense a little ominous dun-dun-dun coming? Well, have a seat because this is where our tried-and-true listen-and-respond leads us astray. For the first time, kids are asking for just one of these things. They just want the listen (at least for a few minutes). They want you to abandon your dynamic duo parenting go-to strategy. They want nothing to do with the respond part, particularly if it involves you teaching a lesson, giving an opinion, or judging what they are saying, thinking, or feeling. They expect you to break up that lovely listen-and-respond marriage that you have relied upon for years. What's really tricky about this is the complete lack of fanfare. There are no flashing neon signs that say, "Mom, Dad, please shut up because this is important to me." That is not going to happen. No friendly public service announcement cluing you in to this shift in the emotional communication jet stream of your parenting dyad. No such luck. So, plenty of parents march along with the expectation that kids want a truly reciprocal exchange leading kids to feel dismissed and shut down. Enter the ominous dun-dun-dun on cue.

Not a win-win. The good news is, you can totally turn things around. Now that you know about this subtle expectation, the nuanced change of choreography in your parent-child tango, you can reassess your approach. Watch the game tapes with a new perspective and all sources of information will point in one direction: Sometimes you will have to break up the listen-and-respond duo.

PUNCTUATION MATTERS

Listening—it's not very hard to do in theory; in fact I'm sure it makes a lot of sense to you. Your son or daughter is growing up and they have something important to say or share. It may have to do with school or friends, an idea they came up with that they are totally jazzed about. It could even deal with things they worry about or stress over. They are coming to you, one of the most important people in their lives, because they want to connect with you. They are willing to bring you on board and they are inviting you to share in their world.

This is not, "Can we get pepperoni on the pizza?" This is more like, "Something is going on in my life and I want you to be a part of it."

Notice anything there? With the punctuation? Right, there's no question mark after the last sentence your child said. They are not asking you for anything, they are inviting you to share in their world. Maybe there is a bit of a roadmap here after all—one we can follow if we pay close attention.

Listen-and-respond works when there is a question, a question mark. Even implied. Listen and respond will not work so well if there's a period (or exclamation point) bringing up the rear.

When our kids invite us to share in their world, when they open their door and welcome us in, they are not necessarily asking for our feedback. They probably do not want our advice or opinion, not just yet. They want to share, and they want to connect. They just want the listen part, not the respond part. They do not want the advice, the opinion, the lecture, or the potential judgment.

Just to make sure we are on the same page, see if these examples make sense. Here are a few things your child may say. The first column, the ones with the question marks are cues for you to listen and respond. The second column contains statements your child may make that are just that, statements. Those are cues for you to just listen (and not offer an opinion, a lecture, etcetera).

Listen & Respond	Just Listen
When will you be home?	I hate when you work late.
Mom, why are the kids so mean to me?	The kids at school were mean today.
How do you make a rocket? Can we?	I have this great idea to make a rocket!

Look at what happens if you give a response, anything more than a single empathetic word or excited exclamation, to the second column. More times than not, you run the risk of judging your child, or launching into a lecture or plan of attack before they even have a chance to get things off their chest or fully explain where they are coming from. Does this example ring any bells?

Your Child Says:

It was awful. All the kids made fun of me and Emily didn't stick up for me and no one helped and I hate all of them. Everyone!

You Probably Want to Say This:

Those girls are the worst, baby—I can't stand them. And Emily does not deserve you. Tomorrow, you are going to march right in there and smile at all of them and go over to Olivia's table and sit there and never look back because they are not worth it!

Or This:

Honey, I really think you're overreacting. Emily's been your best friend since preschool. I can't imagine no one stuck up for you. You know you can be sensitive. Was it really that big a deal? Plus, it's not nice to say you hate them. Hate's a very strong word.

Go ahead; tell her what you really think. I know your intentions are good. I know you know your child better than anyone else and that you see all of her great qualities and growing edges (a.k.a., flaws). I understand your deep seated desire to guide your child away from drama and hurt and potential disaster, and urge her toward wise, well-thought-out choices. But we are grownups and they are kids, and there are times (lots of times) when they need to figure things out on their own. Plus, they probably won't listen to a word you say if they don't feel like you are really listening. Are you longing for the days of the baby monitor yet?

The other thing to take into consideration is that the parental responses in the example don't leave a heck of a lot of room for the child to form her own opinion. Even if she does, if it is not the same as her parent's, well, that's just another conflict to add to the already crummy Tuesday afternoon lineup. No one needs that! By guiding and coaching, or lecturing and preaching, you may unknowingly teach your child that they are better off not coming to you in the first place. I know that is not what anyone wants, but it may be happening more than you know. Here are a few examples, involving things you may never even think to say to your child or possibly things you've uttered, or at least thought. I've included a column reflecting how a child may hear their parent's response, and what it might mean to them.

Child Says	You Might Say	Child Hears
I hate it when you work late.	Honey, I have to work so we have money to do all the things you want to do. OR I'm sorry honey, but that's just the way it is.	WHAT I'M FEELING DOESN'T MATTER TO YOU.
The kids at school were mean today.	What happened!?! OR Did you tell your teacher?	YOU THINK IT'S MY FAULT.
I have this great idea to make a rocket!	A rocket? Really? I'm not sure about that. OR Great, but you have to get your school project done first.	YOU DON'T CARE ABOUT MY IDEA.

We definitely want to get this train back on the tracks and try to keep it there. So let's review what we know: Don't answer questions that your kids don't ask you. Got it, but this may be easier said than done because it requires breaking a habit, inhibiting an impulse. For any parent who has ever said, "Stop doing that!" 372 times in one meal, you appreciate how hard it is to shift a habit or control an impulse. The impulse you need to control is the urge to teach.

As parents, we have to swallow our words and resist the temptation to guide and prompt and ease. We have to quiet down and just listen to what our children are saying without judgment. If and when the urge to fire back comes up, because it may, your job is to find your inner mute button and press it. Press it for dear life. If that does not work, bite the inside of your cheek or the tip of your tongue. Honestly, you may draw blood by the time all of this is said and done, but it will be worth it.

WHAT TO SAY WHEN YOU'RE SAYING NOTHING

We have now cracked the code of communication. You know when to respond and when to pause. You know you may need to literally bite the inside of your lip as the urge to coach and guide and teach intensifies. Does all of this mean you are suddenly speechless and useless? No, not in the least. It does, however, mean that you have to choose your words wisely. I suggest that while you are just listening you say only one word at a time—

maximum two—and only when your child pauses and gives you space to

say it. My thought is that one or two words give you the opportunity to let

them know you are with them, without giving you free reign to formulate a

response (or veer off course into a lecture or opinion!). If you are eye-to-

eye, almost all of this can be done with facial expressions, a nod of the

head, all those great nonverbal methods of connecting. However, if you are

driving and having this exchange within the limited context of your rear-

view mirror or if you're communicating through a freshly slammed

bedroom door, here are some examples you may try on for size:

Your Child Says
It was so bad! All the kids made fun of me and Emily didn't help and I
hate all of them. Everyone!

You Say (Empathetically)
Honey or Term of endearment of your choice OR Aww

Your Child Says
I'm going to make a rocket out of the old lawn mower in the shed!

You Say (Excitedly)
Wow or Sounds cool OR Super idea
(even if you're thinking yikes! and making a note to check your
homeowner's policy)

If this feels a little "eh", I hear you. There is more; it's just a few

pages over. It's called validation and it's the next step in making sure your child feels heard. That said, you can't skip this first step because if you keep moving full steam ahead with listen-and-respond there will be no time or space to validate. Start here by just listening and your child will fill the space and eventually, even if you don't say anything more, he or she will ask a question you can answer.

Seriously, when you tread lightly, pause, and hold back your response, your child will undoubtedly ask you a question. It's as close to magic as I can deliver. When you are communicating with your child and you stop, listen intently, and don't say much of anything for a few minutes while giving your child center stage, he feels a connection that's magnetic. And that allows him to feel confident, to feel that you accept him, and all of a sudden he wants your opinion, your guidance, your feedback. Even if his question is, "Why aren't you saying something!?" you will be given a clear invitation to share at some point.

FINAL THOUGHTS ON CHAPTER 1

Hopefully your ears are ready to accept the challenge of listening and with practice, you'll find that you don't need to chomp down on your cheek quite so hard while waiting for an opportunity to share your thoughts. When you think about it, these tools are just new steps added onto an old, familiar dance. Preschoolers come right out and ask for feedback by saying, "Mommy, Daddy, tell me how to do it." Older kids, they make you earn the opportunity to give guidance because they know they have to be able to figure it out on their own someday.

Now you know about this change up. Now you'll try. Trust me, it will be worth it because getting this under your belt now sets the stage for successful communication when things are much more complicated. When it's not about sleepovers and sharing toys, but about peer pressures, values, and morals. Practice this now so that when things are once again a matter of survival, your kids come to you because they trust that you will truly listen and wait for an invitation to share your sage advice.

Validate:
How to tell your child you get it,
even if you don't

Watch Video Message:
Dr. Stephanie O'Leary Introduces Chapter 2

http://www.stephanieoleary.com/intro-to-
chapter-2-of-parenting-in-the-real-world.html

CHOOSING WORDS WISELY

We just spent some time in the last chapter fine-tuning your parental listening skills. Maybe you have even practiced by holding back a well-intentioned response, opinion, lecture, or judgment, in order to create a more meaningful connection with your child. If so, brilliant, because that is the first step in reducing the level of drama in your parent-child interactions. Plus, it will allow you to talk things out with your son or daughter without the same old conflicts replaying on a seemingly endless loop.

If, however, you are still grappling a bit with how to bite your tongue and swallow your gut reactions and responses, you are in the right place. In this chapter you will learn what to say to keep things calm and productive while navigating conversations, and maybe even potential arguments, with your child. This chapter will help you choose your words wisely after you have given your child a chance to say what she needs to say. You will learn to validate your child's point of view even when you are exhausted, baffled by what you hear, and experiencing an urge to defend yourself. Better yet, you will learn to respond effectively even when you think (or know) that your child is wrong, off base, or completely out of her mind.

This skill is important because it keeps the parent-child connection in place while allowing you to maintain your street cred so that when you finally have a chance to give feedback it does not fall on deaf ears. Let's face it, you have amazing ideas! You can offer well-thought-out suggestions based on a lifetime of experience, but if your child is not ready to hear it, you're wasting your breath.

You learned in the last chapter that listening lays the groundwork for positive outcomes. The next tool on the list is validation, the key to unlocking your child's ears so they can actually hear all the great stuff you're saying.

So what is this validation thing all about? You've heard of it, maybe even thrown the term around now and then, but how does this apply to parenting? And how will it help when dinner is burning, the cat is throwing up, and everyone in your household has disappeared just as the doorbell and two phones begin simultaneously ringing. Validation will help you stop mincing your words and straining your poor vocal cords. It will allow you to talk with your child when he is upset so you can keep things moving in a positive direction and avoid potential disasters.

Validation, simply stated, means to make something valid or to confirm. When you check out at Amazon or your favorite online marketplace, at some point you enter your credit card number and a screen pops up that says validating. It's confirming, or making sure the information you put in matches up with reality. Our iPhones validate our fingerprints before granting us access, our badges/security passes/garage door openers validate entrance to certain spaces, and our signatures validate our intention to keep our word. That's all easy to digest. That's practical validation.

Beyond that though, relationships provide opportunities for validation. You know that it feels good to be acknowledged for your efforts by friends, family members, and coworkers. Even the simplest, "You look nice today," has the potential to bring a smile to your face because it provides validation. Hopefully, as an adult, you validate your own efforts and accomplishments (because after all, the real world can be an unreliable barometer of success). That little, "Heck yeah, I nailed it!" that you whisper to yourself after a brilliant plan comes to life, or the pat on the back you offer yourself for going above and beyond. It's all validation, and it feels darn good.

That warm and fuzzy feeling happens for a reason. When you are validated, it sends the message that you are worthwhile. It leads you to believe that your thoughts, feelings, ideas, and emotions matter. This boosts you up a bit and builds your confidence. To take things a step further, the experience of being validated opens you up a little. Think of the opposite—Jane says, "I have a really great idea!" and the response she gets after her friend listens quietly is, "Well, I'm not so sure about that, but I have this other idea for you." After the friend launches into her newer, better idea, is Jane even listening? Can Jane see straight, or is she seeing red? Is Jane hanging on every last word, or is she questioning why she ever confided in her friend in the first place? Right, Jane basically has her fingers in her ears. Even if her friend offers amazing ideas and feedback, Jane's armor is up. Nothing gets through.

Granted, this is a bit of a dramatization and, for the most part, adults bring more perspective and internal validation to these experiences. That being said, I myself have been in Jane's position, and it did not leave me open to feedback or suggestions. When this happens to children—pre-adolescents and adolescents in particular—they shut down at lightning speed. Children and teens put up their defenses, slap on their armor, and roll up like those little tank bugs, devoting all their energy to self-protection. This usually takes the form of lashing out or shutting down, simply because they were not validated. Kids act out or shrink inward because they feel dismissed. Clearly, this is not productive, especially if your goal is to eventually offer some fantastic guidance and parenting support.

Let's see what happens if you flip things around. Go back to Jane. Remember, she said, "I have a really great idea." This time, her friend listens quietly and then says something along the lines of, "This sounds like it's important to you and you've put a lot of thought into it. I'm glad you're telling me about it." That's different, right? And the friend didn't lie, she didn't say it was a slam-dunk or the best idea ever presented. She validated

that Jane was excited about something and had put a lot of thought into it.

She held up a mirror and reflected back a little bit of what Jane shared, and

she did it nicely. She did it with kindness, and with some empathy. Maybe

she even put herself in Jane's shoes and thought, "What would I want to

hear?" Now, I'm guessing that if and when that same friend offered advice

or constructive feedback, Jane would be in a much better position to hear

it and maybe even accept it. In fact, this friend would probably fall in the

category of one of the "great listeners" we discussed back in Chapter 1

(Listen), someone Jane might seek out for advice and whose opinion she

values. If that's exactly who you want to be for your child, validation is

officially a must-have for your parenting toolbox.

One final note here before we dive into the nitty-gritty. The most

important opportunities for validation come in like gale-force winds. They

happen when your child experiences strong emotions. It doesn't matter if

it's extreme elation and joy or utter despair and anger. Any time the

emotional pendulum swings more than a few degrees past neutral,

validation should take front and center. This makes sense because when

our emotions are neutral, the circumstances are pretty run-of-the-mill and

things don't seem to matter all that much. When emotions intensify, the

stakes automatically rise. Parents know this. The negative stuff is easy to spot, and you have seen firsthand how quickly excitement and joy can tip

the scales into hysteria. So when your child comes to you (or at you,

because sometimes that's how it feels), and you pick up on big emotions,

stop dead in your tracks. Listen. Pause (potentially while literally biting your

tongue). Validate.

LISTEN.

Pause.

VALIDATE.

I wish there were a catchy acronym to go along with this set of

tools but, alas, there's not. So you'll listen (without saying more than one or

two words). You'll pause for a few seconds until you sense a lull in the

emotion or until you're bordering on awkward silence, and then you will

bust out your best attempt at validation.

SAY WHAT?!?

Let's break validation down so you can start to practice. The typical old

way of responding to your child goes something like this:

Child:
Blah blah blah blah blah!

You:
Well, honey, what about bleh bleh bleh?
OR
Really? Seriously? Rant, rant, rant, rave, rave, rave, judge, judge, judge,
and possibly lecture, lecture, lecture.

In real life, maybe it's more like this. Or maybe it was just like this last

week in my house. Either way:

Child:
We have to hand in our foreign language choices tomorrow and I have to
take French. I have to! We go to France in high school and I know
you want me to take Mandarin but that's not even a guaranteed
class so I already chose French so please just sign it.

You:
Well, honey, we've talked about this and both Daddy and I feel like
Mandarin is the best choice. When are you ever gonna use French
anyway? And who says you're going to France?

OR

Are you freakin' kidding me!? We have been over this 100 times. Why in
the world did you fill out the sheet when you know we've discussed this!
Seriously, nine o'clock at night is not a good time to have this
conversation. I'm done.

Both of these parent responses are not so validating. Both send a clear message to the child—what you want does not matter. Both convey that taking French is not acceptable, not practical, and a plain old bad idea, and the child winds up feeling as if his or her desire to take French is not worthwhile.

Here, it's important to clarify that validation is not about something being right or wrong. I'm willing to bet you are very good at validating things that you understand and naturally feel empathetic about, but nowhere on these pages will you read that your child has to be right in order for you to validate them. That's insane, because kids are wrong lots of the time. Even still, they need to be validated so you can get on to the part where you offer wise perspectives they just might accept. As a parent, you will not always steer your child's ship and be in charge of their every move. In reality, you want your child to figure some of this life *stuff* out on his own. Validating your child right off the bat instead of trying to shove your ideas down his agitated throat will allow him to take what you say into consideration. Remember, you want your child to keep his fingers far away from his ears so he can actually hear you. After all, you do know what you're talking about!

If you need a spoon full of sugar to help digest this, here's a little dose of self-disclosure that may put things in perspective. The example I gave, the French situation, is my real life. One of the parent responses was what I was thinking. The other was what I actually said. Wait, what!? I didn't listen, pause, validate? No my friends, I did not. I am also a work in progress, and I'm going to give myself props for not saying what I was actually thinking (although there are times when that happens as well).

Just thought I'd throw in this friendly reminder because I have been in the parenting boat, the same one you are in. We're all paddling together. I still think Mandarin makes more sense than French, but I'm willing to compromise if we can talk about it calmly because, at the end of the day, it's way more important to me that my daughter learns to advocate for her needs and tolerate feedback that may be hard to hear than if she crams for the French or Mandarin final in four years. Big picture, it's not always about the outcome, it's about the process. And validation makes that process far more productive.

Now, back to work. Using the tools you've learned so far—listen, pause, and validate—the conversation would go like this, just substitute a common household rant (this isn't fair, I'm so upset about something, you don't listen to me—for the "Blah, blah, blah" part):

Child: Blah, blah, blah, blah, blah!

You Listen/Say One Word: Wow (said with interest)
                                              OR
                                              Oh (said empathetically)

Child: Yeah! Blah, blah, blah, blah, blah!

You Listen/Say One Word: Yeah (said with interest)
                                              OR
                                              Aww (said empathetically)

Child: Yeah, blah, blah, blah, blah, blah!

You Listen/Say One Word: OK (said with interest)
                                              OR
                                              Term of endearment of your choice
                                              (said empathetically ... my personal
                                              faves being love and baby,
                                              sometimes combined into the
                                              super-powered baby-love)

[Repeat however many times it takes.]

Child: (silence)

You Validate: It sounds like blah, blah, blah,
                                              blah. Blah, blah, blah sounds
                                              hard/great/frustrating/whatever it
                                              might be.

Child: I KNOW! Blah, blah, blah, blah.
                                              What do I do?

You Respond: (FINALLY!) Offer opinion, guide,
                                              offer support.

In real life, possibly in my house last week, the conversation might go

something like this:

Child:	We have to hand in our foreign language choices tomorrow and I have to take French. I have to! We go to France in high school and I know you want me to take Mandarin but that's not even a guaranteed class so I already chose French so please just sign it.
You Listen/Say One Word:	Oh (said empathetically)
Child:	Yeah, I HAVE to take French! PLEASE!
You Listen/Say One Word:	Babe (said empathetically)
Child:	MOM! (followed by silence)
You Validate:	Sounds like French is really important to you, it must be frustrating that Daddy and I want you to take Mandarin.
Child:	Yeah. Exactly! What are we gonna do?
You Respond:	Well, we can talk again and see if there's a compromise we can all live with. Plus, we have some time because the sheet is actually due back on Friday. How about we talk tomorrow night after dinner and figure this out.
Child:	Okay (grumpily)

This same conversation will take place in a million different ways, involving a million different topics, each covering a whole bunch of emotions and agendas. What will help you most is to stick to the basics—the listen, pause, validate framework, your new go-to parenting script.

Let's break it down a bit to make sure things are crystal clear. The key to successful validation is to be empathic and reflect back a little of what your child is saying. For example, if your child comes at you with a whole bunch of grumps, groans, and maybe even shouts and tears, you might try, "Honey, it sounds like today was disappointing." If you can't make sense of anything she is saying, keep it simple and stick with being empathetic, "That sounds tough." Then, when your child calms down a bit you can offer assistance. You can ask, "Do you want hear what I think?" Or, "Do you want to try to make a plan together?" This last part may not happen right away, it may take a few minutes, hours, even days, but the opportunity to partner with your child will come, and when it does your words will not fall on deaf ears stuffed with defensive little fingers.

If you were in my office or having a consultation call with me, this is the point where I would ask you to tell me about the three most common fights, conflicts, arguments, that take place in your home. I would ask you to share exactly what your child says, and then I would give you the validating words to reflect back, but modern technology has only come so far. Since we are limited to words on the written page for now, you can think about the three most common conflicts that you have with your child. Think really hard about what your child says, and what they come to you, or at you, with. Try not to dwell on what you usually say back to your child, just stop and think about how you might be able to validate what they are experiencing and expressing. **Validation** = Empathy + A little of what they said—*if you can make sense of it.*

Here are some examples of validating statements:

Child Says: My teacher is totally unfair. He never tells us what to study and the tests are way too hard!

Validate: That sounds tough. Feeling like you can't prepare must stink.

Child Says: I'm going to the movies this weekend and then sleeping over at Sean's house. Then on Saturday I'm going to the game and I also need to go to the mall, okay?

Validate: Sounds like you have a lot of plans for the weekend.

Child Says: I hate it that you and Mommy fight all the time. I can't handle it.

Validate: Babe, it must be so hard to hear us fighting.

Child Says: No one ever listens to me or cares about what I say. I don't even matter. I wish I wasn't even part of this family!

Validate: I'm sorry it feels like no one cares.

I'm going to be honest. This is not easy. It's a tall order to stop in the midst of all that your child brings to the table, find a shred of what he's saying that you can relate to, and reflect it back in the form of validation. Oh yeah, and don't forget to be empathic, even if your child is screaming.

To make things a bit more complicated, these conversations don't happen in isolation. In fact, it seems as if kids choose the most inopportune times to bring up emotional topics, like when you are in the middle of at least six other things, two of which might result in bodily harm if not executed carefully. Your child will rarely come to you when you are clear headed, well rested, and sitting back staring at a completed to-do list. Actually, you may never be in that state, but if you were, these emotionally laden conversations, ripe with conflict, probably would not present themselves. Your child will most likely approach you with intense emotion and a lot to say just when you are least prepared. You will still try to listen, pause, and validate, because you know it will get you and your child moving in the right direction.

BUT THAT'S CRAZY!

You're right. Sometimes the things your child says or expresses may seem, for lack of a better word, crazy. I'm not kidding. I believe that every parent, at one time or another has seriously called into question their child's grasp on reality. It's all part of growing up. Things are changing incredibly fast as brains and bodies grow at warp speed. Then, at a certain age you add hormonal shifts to the mix and it's amazing that anyone is able to face the world. Throughout this developmental process you will be called upon to validate thoughts, feelings, and ideas that make no sense at all. You will be asked to do this even when you disagree with what your child is doing, saying, or thinking.

So, when your child comes to you with seeming nonsense, things like, "Billy said he got $1000 from the tooth fairy and I didn't. That's not fair and I hate you!" Or, "Seriously, you told me I could go yesterday. When you were making dinner you told me I could sleep over at Megan's even though her parents are away. YOU PROMISED!" Or, "No one ever reads to me. You always read to Dylan and you *never* read to me!" Your job isn't to lie to your child or agree with her to make her feel better. Your job is to validate her experience, have empathy, and reflect back what she's throwing at you. If your child says something you can't wrap your head around, try one of these one-liners (while carefully avoiding sarcasm):

I hear you; it's hard.

This totally stinks.

I'm sorry you feel that way.

No lying. You did hear your child. And yes, clearly it is hard. It does totally stink. You probably are sorry your child is upset because things would be easier all around if they weren't! These simple, validating sentences will help you avoid an emotional argument and keep you in the game until your child is able to calm down. Better still, using one of these validating statements will leave the door open for your child to come back to you, trust you, and even listen to what you have to say.

I KNOW; IT'S HARD

We've established that validating can be hard, but does it work? Well, that's always the million-dollar question, right? Does this work? Will it help? Is it worth it? Back when I started my career as a psychologist, before I was a mother, I always felt like a bit of a fraud because I didn't practice what I taught. I had no children of my own. I was not facing the same real-life situations that parents were and when they earnestly asked me, "Will this make a difference?" the best I could offer was my educated vote of confidence.

It's been a while since I began my clinical work, and I have certainly logged my fair share of parenting hours. At this point, I can say without hesitation that the listen, pause, validate strategy truly makes a difference. Will it result in a zero-conflict household? No. Will it have you and your children communicating like polite puppets in a school talent show? No. Will it turn the volume down on the drama? Yes. Will it eventually, with practice, create an amazing shift in your relationship with your child? Yes, I know that it will.

Here's how I know. I have two very different children. I do my best every day to use the strategies and tools I'm sharing with you in this book. I do not do this perfectly, or every single time, but there is a concerted effort. To give you some context, my children have big personalities and lots of intense ideas, thoughts, and emotions. Since birth, they have each had a lot going on, and I think it's important to share with you how I've used validation, and how it keeps that door open for me to connect with my kids, even when it's hard and messy.

I'll start with my little guy, my practical, maybe even pragmatic, son who has a sharp mind and a quick wit. From a very early age, I knew that the listen, pause, validate approach worked for him because he turned it right around and used it on me (that little bugger!). He was the preschooler who would say things like, "Mommy, I know you're tired and you said we don't have time to read tonight, but I just wanted to say it makes me sad because I love reading with you." Dude, you just listened, validated, and totally upped the ante by telling me how you're feeling! I get it, kids are great at getting their needs met, but who's the Jedi master now, right? Needless to say, my son got some books read to him even though it was late and we were all beyond tired.

Just the other day, during a not-so-spectacular parenting moment when I let my general frustration level get the best of me, my son busted out with, "I know you're upset about the dogs, but don't yell." Certainly, it's not my child's job to validate me, but I always take note because kids do as we do, and I'm guessing on some level he throws those statements in because that's the way he is used to being spoken to. He uses the same strategies to communicate that he hears me using with him, and at the end of the day, I think that's pretty awesome because they work.

Now my oldest, the little girl who taught me to be a mom, is a very different child. She used to have intense, drop-down, fall-out tantrums as a preschooler. Not all the time, but at least a few times a month. I had seen my way around a tantrum or two before parenthood while working in daycares and preschools, but my daughter took things to the next level. For example, instantaneously getting upset about something while walking from the car to the mall and suddenly deciding to flee from us (my husband and me) to run frantically around the parking lot, at night, in Westchester, NY, in January. More than one bystander offered to call for help (whatever that meant). It was not good. On more than one occasion, she dumped out entire dresser drawers and flipped bookshelves. You get the picture.

Throughout each tantrum, lots of words and emotions (and grunts, and shouts, and screams) were spewed. I, we, tried everything we could think of to get things—to get her—back under control. This included asking, begging, even shouting at her to stop. Trying to reason with her. Offering bribes. You name it, we tried it. And then one day, one particularly rough day when I was about 35 weeks pregnant, a major meltdown hit. I felt exhausted. My husband gave it his all and then started to lose it himself, so I was called into the arena. I felt so spent that I did something different. My daughter, my precious, lovable, bright, joyful little three-and-a-half-year-old was screaming and just shy of scratching her own skin off. I wanted to cry, but instead I said, "I know baby girl, it's hard." She kept going, and I kept saying that, and just that, over and again. I meant it, because it was hard.

Honestly, I had no idea what she was saying or what had set things off in the first place, but if I knew one thing in that moment, it was *this is hard*. Without knowing what the heck I was doing, I validated. Trust me, it was not a like a scene from Harry Potter where someone recites a magical spell and everything falls into place. However, my daughter did something new. She eventually stopped, slowed down, paused, looked up at me with huge, tear-filled eyes, and said, "Hold me." I held her, she let me, and she calmed down.

That was a game changer for me. From then on, when those emotional hurricanes blew in, I hunkered down with my mantra, "I know. This is hard." Each time she eventually allowed me help her. As she's grown up, the hurricanes come much less frequently, but to this day, if and when they do pull into port, my mantra is the same: I know. This is hard.

In retrospect, after having recovered from approximately seven years of sleep deprivation and gaining some clarity, I know what happened. My daughter was having all sorts of emotions that she could not cope with. She did the best she could, and she brought those intense emotions to me.

Once I got out of my own way and stopped trying to hold her, calm her, change her, and teach her, once I simply met her where she was and threw a little empathy her way, she fell into my arms and let me help.

Without a doubt, it was a labor of love because watching her struggle while fighting the urge to fix things was painful. I felt helpless. I probably felt a lot like she did, but parents will do anything for their kids once they have a clue. To this day, when I'm tuned in and brave enough to meet my daughter where she is, validate, and tell her I know it's hard, she eventually falls into my arms. It never ceases to amaze me that on these occasions, probably the most tumultuous our home sees, I am overwhelmed with joy and eternally grateful that she lets me in, that she lets me help her, and love her, and support her.

There are countless other times when things escalate to what I would call the thunderstorm level (you know, run of the mill outbursts, conflicts, etc.), and when listen, pause, validated is used, my little girl grumbles her way through it. Amazingly, in the last year or so she has started coming to me minutes or even hours later saying something along the lines of, "I'm really sorry I acted that way. I was just upset."

I truly almost fell out of my chair the first time it happened. We were on our way to a music lesson and—for some reason—plans had changed and we would have to make a pit stop on the way home. As soon as my daughter caught wind of this she launched into a tirade about how it wasn't fair, it couldn't happen, and how no one cared about what she needs or wants (you get the gist). It was a 15-minute car ride and she was on a 15-minute rant. I gave my few sensitive one-word responses, as well as my tried-and-true validation for her: I know it's hard. There was some tense silence, but she gave it one last go as she slammed the car door and stormed into her lesson.

Thirty minutes later she came back, got in the car and said, "Mom, I'm really sorry I got so upset, it's just hard for me when plans change."

My mind was blown. Blown! That's full circle. That's the whole point—for kids to be able to sort out their own thoughts and emotions so they can communicate and self-advocate. How did I respond to this groundbreaking turn of events? I didn't rehash what had happened, or get into a deep conversation with my daughter. I did not call her out on all the intense (potentially irrational) things she had said. I said, "Thanks babe, I know that was hard," and I meant it.

FINAL THOUGHTS ON CHAPTER 2

Now that you know about the power of validation, I hope that you'll give it a try, and keep trying even when it's hard. Validation unlocks the door for you to give feedback, to guide, coach, and support. Better yet, validation accomplishes all of this while creating mutual respect. You listen to your child, you validate them, and they will be more likely to listen to and validate you. Crazy, I know, but it works like a charm.

Remember, don't freak out if you struggle here. Validating can be challenging. It requires practice, slip-ups, and course corrections. Trust me, your child will provide ample opportunity for you to rehearse. So listen, pause, validate, and let your child amaze you.

CHAPTER 3

Respect:
Because what goes around
comes around

Watch Video Message:
Dr. Stephanie O'Leary Introduces Chapter 3

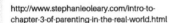

http://www.stephanieoleary.com/intro-to-
chapter-3-of-parenting-in-the-real-world.html

I can't imagine writing a parenting book without talking about respect.
There's not a chance that I would skip this topic because it is near and dear
to every parent's heart. I often hear from families about their collective
desire for more respect at home. Think about it—aren't you longing to
hear a respectful tone of voice or a respectful request? I'm sure even a
respectful refusal would be a welcome change. Respect plays a huge role
within households because it sets the stage for how family members treat
each other, and being respectful is an invaluable life skill.

When you display respect, you inherently do a better job of communicating and getting your needs met. This is common sense. If you ask a question respectfully, you are more likely to receive a response. Better yet, you are more likely to hear an answer you're happy with. If you have to provide feedback and you do it respectfully, not only are you more likely to make your point, but your words somehow carry more weight. Respect is a powerful tool. No wonder we parents want more of it from our kids and for our families.

PUMP UP THE RESERVOIR OF RESPECT

Like many of the things we have explored, the best way to increase the level of respect within your household is to start with yourself. I know it would be much easier if we made it all about the kids, but you have complete control over what you do and say, and how you do and say it. Stepping into that power provides an amazing opportunity to model and teach respect on a daily basis while doing nothing more than going about your same old routine. Respect is not about doing more or less, but about going through your day differently. Thoughtfully.

By keeping just two simple things in mind, accurate word choice and conveying kindness, you will begin to ramp up the respect level in your home. Then you can sit back, cross your fingers, and watch as the contagious effect of respect spreads. The theory is that by observing your respectful actions and choices, your child will begin to take similarly respectful actions and make similarly respectful choices. All the while, you're sending the message to your child that she deserves respect, and that she is a worthwhile individual. Your child will swallow this message whole. I've seen it happen in my house and I've heard children tell me about it in session after session. Even when you think your child is not listening, she is, and children tend to believe what parents say, despite their rebuttals and retorts. The reality is, your child believes what you say even if you don't really mean it and even if they don't want to hear it.

This is an incredible concept. When you stop and think, you'll see how much power you have and how much responsibility comes with that power (almost in the words of the great Jedi master himself!). The way you ask your child what he wants for lunch, the words you choose when giving him feedback about his homework, the tone you project when talking with him about his friends, ideas, or plans—those actions have a deep and profound impact. Saying, "Shut up for one second and please, PLEASE tell me what you want for lunch before I lose it," sends a very different message than, "I know you're excited about this story—real quick, can you just tell me what you want for lunch tomorrow, so I can make sure we have what you need?" Both statements ask the exact same question, and it doesn't take a therapist to pick up on the fact that each sends a vastly different message.

When you convey respect while talking with your child, your child learns that he or she deserves respect. In turn, your child is more likely to give respect—to you and to others. Moreover, your good intentions will provide a source of ongoing, internal support. Your show of respect for your child will create a reservoir of resilience that he can tap into for the rest of his life. This means that even when you're not there, your love and respect continue to have a positive influence.

Think about this. When your child is trying to recover from an insult at the lunch table, staring at a poor test grade, being clobbered by a social disappointment, or grappling with any number of tumbles and falls that are inevitably part of growing up, he or she will dip right into that reservoir (the one that you helped fill up), and will drink up the feeling of being worthwhile, of being plenty good enough. Your child will feel certain that he deserves respect because you respected him. You will teach your child this lesson by showing respect day in and day out.

This "do as I do" cycle is real, and it is incredibly powerful. Please hold onto this notion and use it as a source of motivation as you begin to think about the ways you can tweak your daily routine to raise the volume on respect. As a parent living in the real world, I know that even when you try your best, you may not hit it out of the park every time. There will be fouls and fumbles, and sometimes the ball will drop all together. That's okay. You'll keep trying.

As you practice, the concept of respectful communication will become second nature to you for a few reasons. First, you'll be repeating yourself less and making choices you feel proud of (does less guilt sound good to you?). Plus, when you use these concepts in your daily routine, I'm certain that your children will toss more respect in your direction, both in what they say, or don't say, and in what they do, or don't do. So you'll try to practice respect, and if you have a moment where you are not kind, or when you do not choose words that accurately reflect your intention, you'll own it, repair it (by apologizing and meaning it ... refer to Chapter 5: Be Accountable), and move right on to trying again. Every parent, every person is a work in progress, so respect yourself as you start to make these changes. Dip into your own internal reservoir of confidence whenever you need to. It's worth it, and your child is counting on you.

SAY WHAT YOU MEAN TO SAY:

PARENTING RESPECT TOOL #1

I mentioned that there are two tools you will use to help increase the level of respect in your household. The first is word choice. Creating clear, accurate communication by choosing words that convey exactly what you're trying to say is critical. This cuts down on confusion, and also ensures that you and your child have the same information, that you're both on the same page. Without clear and accurate communication, it is far too easy for you to feel disrespected. It unfolds like this: You feel you have said something and your child is not following through or responding, but you didn't actually say what you thought you said in the first place so your child never had a chance to follow through!

I'll give you one of my favorite examples. Lots of times parents will say something along the lines of this to a child, "Honey, do you want to come have dinner?" Or, "Jake, you wanna go get your PJs on?" Or, "Lily, do you want to come take a bath?" And then, the child will respond by decidedly not doing the thing that was suggested, as evidenced by complete inaction or a flat out "no." More often than not, a parent in this situation will interpret their child's response as being disrespectful. Parents perceive they are being ignored or dismissed, and this is not helpful for anyone.

Do you see the problem in the examples I gave? Those moms, dads, and caregivers asked questions. They approached their child and presented what looked to me like a choice, an option to do something or not do something. I get it. Those parents were probably exhausted or overwhelmed, or maybe just not paying a whole lot of attention to the words they chose. I am absolutely sure they knew what they meant to say. They meant to say, "It's time to come to dinner, it's time to get your PJs on, and it's time to take a bath." Those are the things parents want to see happen, but those are not the things they asked for.

Another prime example is when you say our child's name, but with a tone that implies something else. You know this game, and it can even be played with a term of endearment. Change which syllable you stress, the inflection you use, or your volume and a simple "Stephen" or "Victoria" can mean anything from "I'm so proud of you," to "Stop that right now," to "Hurry up, we're late and I'm going to lose my mind if we don't leave right now," or even "I'm warning you—if you don't put your plate in the sink like I've asked you to 17 times already I'm never making you waffles again."

I'm sure you see that the words parents use do not always match up with what they mean to communicate to their child, and if parental statements do not reflect parental intention, kids never have a chance to follow through. In the end, we wind up with a ticked-off parent and a confused kid. That's definitely not a great way to start dinner or bedtime or whatever else is on the docket, so choosing words wisely is important.

Practicing this skill requires a bit of effort up front because some of your ingrained habits will need changing. You will need to pay attention to statements you make while in autopilot mode, but you will practice, you will make a point to say what you mean to say. This means you'll be honest. Sometimes your child will not like what you're saying, but that's not the point. Nowhere in this discussion of respect will you see a vow to keep everyone happy all of the time. Remember, we're doing this in the real world, with real expectations.

While honing your "accuracy in communication" skills, imagine sending your statements through a fictional truth scanner to see if anything is being lost in translation. If you find that there is something you're about to say that is not accurate, kick it to the curb and start again. You can even correct yourself. If you've said something that you quickly realize is not accurate, give yourself a redo and communicate your message clearly. Case in point, if you slip and say, "You're seriously playing video games?!" Redo the entire exchange by saying aloud, "That's not what I meant to say, I meant to say please go put your soccer stuff away now." Being accurate with your word choice means that you have to be accountable for what you want and what you are asking of your children. That's a good thing. It will make you think about what you expect and allow you to give your son or daughter a chance to hear you and respond. Here are some more examples of things you might say that don't really communicate what you mean, and quick revisions that will allow you to communicate your message clearly:

Examples When Things Get Lost in Translation	Clear Communication "What I meant to say was ..."
Do you want to come to the store?	We need to leave for the store in five minutes. I'll meet you in the car.
Are you kidding me? I can't believe you're still sitting in front of the TV!	I'm upset because you didn't go upstairs when your show ended. Turn the TV off right now and go to bed.
It's so nice out today. Wouldn't it be great if we took a family hike later?	We're all taking a family hike at 2:30 and we'll be home by 3:45. Just wanted to give you a heads-up so you can plan around it.

When you use clear communication, if and when your child does

not follow through, you can call them on it (with kindness of course). Let's

take one of the examples from above and see it through:

Parent:	Are you kidding me? I can't believe you're still in front of the TV!
Child:	Oh, sorry. I forgot.
Parent (Redo):	What I meant to say was I'm upset because you didn't go upstairs when your show ended. Turn the TV off right now and go to bed.
Child:	Mom! (Said while continuing to stare at TV).
Parent:	What do you need to be doing?
Child:	Ugh, can't I just finish this show? It's almost over.
Parent:	If you turn off the TV now and go to bed you can have your show tomorrow. If I have to turn the TV off, you'll lose that privilege. It's your choice.
Child:	That's so unfair! (Said while turning the TV off and going upstairs).

You clearly and accurately communicated your request so there's

no excuse for your child not to know what you expect. Maybe there are

potato farms in her ears and she needs you to repeat yourself. Okay, you

can roll with that. You'll repeat yourself once so there is no possible

misunderstanding and even follow up with a potential consequence or repercussion if needed. This will lead to compliance, even if it's begrudging at first, and once you and your child are speaking the same language you will quickly notice the respect level increase.

KINDNESS MATTERS: PARENTING RESPECT TOOL #2

You have heard it said a million times that it's not what you say, but how you say it that matters. Well, I think I've made it clear that what you say as a parent is pretty darn important, but the way you say it matters a whole lot, too. When it comes to respectful communication, delivering well-thought-out statements, requests, and questions in a kind fashion is key. Wrapping words up in kindness is the other half of the respect equation, and while use of this tool will also take practice, it is usually much easier to get the hang of. Choosing words involves a lot of moving pieces, so many words to consider, so many things you want to say. This side of the coin, speaking with kindness, is a one shot deal. You get to practice the exact same thing over and again, allowing you to create a new, productive habit quickly.

Let's take this step-by-step, starting from where you are right now. When you think about the level of kindness you display within your household, on a scale from one to ten, where do things fall? Think about

the kindness "climate" and see what temperature comes to mind. Clearly,

there will be fluctuations, but overall where do you see things falling?

Chances are you don't need to reflect for long to come up with an

answer. I bet you know how kind you are to your children and other family

members, and I would venture a guess that it does change depending on

how you feel, your own stress level, and the current demands being placed

on you. That all makes sense, and I think it's safe to say we are all in that

same boat once again. Just for good measure though, see if you can size up

the low and high points of your home's kindness range, the floor and

ceiling, so to speak. Think carefully about how things look when there is a

real lack of kindness, and also try to capture and appreciate the landscape

when the kindness is flowing. Now tell me, or tell yourself, which feels

better, floor or ceiling? Where do you see you and your child getting more

of what you want, floor or ceiling? Where do you feel like the parent you

want to be, floor or ceiling? Right, ceiling. It's much more productive,

comfortable, and possibly even joyful up at the level where more kindness,

and respect, circulate.

This self-reflective exercise is important because it forces you to

take your blinders off and see things as they are. Hopefully, you were able to think of some wonderful parenting moments, times when you went above and beyond to make sure you were sensitive, to go that extra mile for your child, to insert a little humor or linger in your hug just a few seconds longer. You turned up the song he likes, slipped the note into her lunch, looked at his eyes when you complimented his efforts, showed up when you thought you couldn't. I know these things happen in most every home, and that well-intentioned parents have the capacity to be the kindest creatures in the world. Hang onto these instances and see if you can stretch them out, serve them up more frequently, and make a point to prioritize kindness when interacting with your child.

How about times when kindness was lacking, or maybe even completely absent? Maybe you used a cutting—or a harsh, or even frightening tone. The scowl, eye roll, or grimace accompanying your words may have completely changed their meaning. The sarcasm you dished out may have ultimately served the purpose of chipping away at your child's self-esteem. These things happen too, and sadly, as your child matures and starts using her words and voice to tell you what she thinks, you may even feel justified in your lack of kindness. You may also start seeing these same harsh behaviors thrown right back at you. Please know that you are the grown up, the adult, the one who invited the tiny human to the party in the first place. Your child didn't ask to come live at your house, but you're in it together now. As a parent, you have to commit to putting your big-girl or big-boy pants on every day and practice taking the high road.

What does that high road look like, you might ask? Well, let's talk about all the things you won't see in the vista while traveling the high road. There's no name calling. No stupid, dummy, freak, or loser. There are no b-words, or f-words, or a/h-words (are you with me?). In fact, there are no curses. No shut-ups. There is no belittling, bullying, making or poking fun at. There is no scaring others on purpose, intimidating, or threatening. These are things that parents do when they are out of control. These things create chaos and sap joy from a household in the blink of an eye or slam of a fist. Clearly, these things do not fall under the umbrella of kindness. In all honesty, I'm not one for focusing on the negative, but it's important to be real here and I need to cover all these bases so there's no confusion. These things do not fall under another heading or topic; they represent a complete lack of kindness and therefore a complete lack of respect. I'm a pretty flexible person, but there is no wiggle room here. These things are off limits, and if they show up or sneak in, you, as the parent, can get back to the high road quickly by owning your misstep and repairing your communication (again, see Chapter 5; Be Accountable).

If you feel there are so many of these unkind words and behaviors in your home that you doubt your ability to make a change, I'm glad you're being honest with yourself. I'm also sure there's a reason for all the harshness and chaos, and that reason might run deep. If you are nodding your head frantically or tearing up here, please give yourself permission to get some support. Read Chapter 7 (Self Care for Parents), and take care of yourself so you can be there for your kids.

If you know there is definite room for improving the level of kindness in your house, and you feel like you have the internal resources to try it a different way, let's look at some practical tools that can help. First off, keep in mind that your children will likely seek out partners in life who treat them as you do. They will likely attract and be attracted to partners who speak to them the way you speak to them. Know that as you open your mouth and speak your mind. The way you talk to your daughter, that's how she will expect to be treated by her partners. The way you speak to your son, that's how he will expect to be treated by his partners, and how he will likely speak to them. I'm sharing this idea not to scare you, but to empower you as you move toward kindness and respect.

Do not call your sons and daughters names that you would not want their future significant others to call them. Do not treat your sons and daughters in any way that you would not want to see their future significant other treat them. Think on that for a minute. Think about you, at your worst, speaking to your child. Now, flash forward a few years, and imagine that it's not you spewing those words, but a boyfriend or girlfriend. How would you react? What would you do? Would a 9-1-1 call or fistfight be on tap? Right, because you are supposed to want to protect your child. Now, step back into the real world and remember, it was you coming at your child in the first place. Do not mistake this reality flash for judgment. That's a cop out. This is real world stuff, food for thought, and a wake-up call so you can start to make important and powerful changes right now. Here are some suggestions:

KIND & HONEST STATEMENTS:

- I'm frustrated with this situation.

- I know we're both upset, but I don't want to fight.

- I'm too upset to talk right now. I'm going to take ten minutes to try to calm down.

- I'm having a hard time controlling my anger right now so I need to take a break.

So, what do you do if you feel your kindness slipping and you can't regroup or find something appropriate to say? One great strategy is to stop. Just stop. Stop talking. Stop participating. Give yourself a time out. Leave the room, go to your room, just take yourself out of the situation in any way possible. It is far better to say nothing, to bow out for a bit, than to say or do something unkind. You have complete permission to take a time out, and—let's face it—at a certain point you really can't send your kids there anymore so you might as well take advantage of this great tool yourself!

If things are not that far off the tracks and you don't feel the need to take a breather, you can try to use one of my favorite parenting tools— shrinking. Shrink your hand movements, your facial expressions, and your physical presence. Take an actual step backward, away from the exchange. Lower your voice to a whisper. All of these actions communicate something intentional. They send the message that you are not a threat. When someone approaches you, comes at you, gesticulates and shouts, it puts you on the defensive. This same thing happens for children, especially for teens. In contrast, when someone steps away, lowers their hands, neutralizes their face, and begins to whisper, defenses are dropped because the sense of threat instantaneously dissipates. That's powerful. Plus, when you yell at your child during the course of a conversation or exchange, his general response is to cover his ears or shrug his shoulders (which in essence sort of covers his ears), and turn away. When you whisper during the course of a conversation, your child will tend to lean in and turn his head toward you to ensure he can hear as much of what you say as possible. Based on these patterns, not only will lowering your voice lead you back to the high road of kindness, it will also improve the odds of your child hearing your words and your message. And your voice will be spared. Win-win.

All of the information from Chapter 2 (Validation) lays the groundwork for communicating respectfully and kindly with your child. When you validate, you send the message that you care about your child's perspective. You may not agree, but you are taking the time to consider his ideas and opinions. In case you are reading the book out of order and have not been through Chapter 2 yet, here's the cheat sheet. Before you launch into whatever it is you want your child to hear (according to what we covered here, that would be your carefully chosen words that communicate exactly what you want to have happen next), stop and say something empathic to your child, such as, "I know this is hard" or, "I hear that you're excited about that." Reflect whatever is relevant to your current situation or conversation. This validation serves to connect you with your child so she is more apt to hear what you have to say.

Another great tool to use is asking your child to look you in the eye while you talk to him. This not only increases the likelihood of him hearing you, but can also provide a humorous "setup" for whatever you are about to say. This is one of my personal favorites, maybe because it lets me be a bit of a goofball, but also because it works like a charm. The setup definitely gets a child's attention. For example, you could say in a joking voice, "Look at me for a sec because I have something totally crazy to say—you're gonna think I've completely lost my mind!" Or, you could say jokingly, "Can you look at me really quick, I'm going to say something you're not going to like at all—it's totally a bummer!" Then, you deliver your carefully chosen words. Something like, "Please take out the trash," or, "Please come to the table and do your math homework." Set them up with a kind, joking intro so your words don't fall on deaf ears and so you are not screaming your head off and feeling like a disrespected (and disrespectful) parent.

When it comes to kindness, keep it simple. Be nice; don't be mean. Talk to you kids the way you want other people to talk to them. If you have to, pretend they're not your kids for a minute. Talk to them like they're kids you're babysitting. You'll probably be much nicer without even trying that hard. If you are unkind, own it, repair it (details on this to follow in Chapter 5; Be Accountable), and get right back on the high road again. Take this one step at a time, and keep things moving in a respectful direction.

ASK FOR WHAT YOU WANT

Now that you have a solid grasp on how to communicate with your child respectfully, there is another simple tool you can use. You see, after you have shown him or her what it feels like when people say what they mean to say and do so kindly, you can start to ask for that same treatment in return. This is not complicated and it works like magic. Let's say, hypothetically, your child says something that is neither respectful nor kind. Something like, "Eww, dinner smells gross," or, "Mom, I told you I didn't want you to do that! Ugh!!" (I'm sure you can conjure up some of your very own examples here.) When your child makes one of these statements you can now say in a neutral tone of voice, "Please say that again respectfully." If he looks at you like you have two heads, that's fine. This is a new thing for everyone. Don't take the bait and launch into a tirade on how awful he is and how hard you're working to be respectful (because that's shooting yourself in the foot). Let him stare at you or even laugh or roll his eyes. You will not respond until he can make a respectful statement. At times, it helps to give a child the words. If your child can't get there on her own you can say, "It's respectful to say, 'What's for dinner mom?'" In the end, if you can respond to your child's not-so-respectful statements with kindness and accuracy, you can also hold her accountable for improving her own behavior.

Here, you may be wondering how to react if your child displays a more intense level of disrespect (cursing, repeated rude or inappropriate comments, even hitting, kicking, etc.). The kindness tool is still important and anything you say will be most impactful if it is delivered without name-calling, threats, or intimidation. That being said, you, as the parent, can communicate in a serious tone while still being respectful and accurate in your word choice. This is important to keep in mind as you start setting limits and boundaries (covered in the next chapter), because practicing kindness does not mean that you are a pushover or that you'll tolerate or dismiss your child's inappropriate behavior. In contrast, when you start using these tools and making respect a priority, you will expect more in return from your children. Once they go out on a limb and start trying to follow your example, children will quickly learn that you respond to them much more positively. They will see that this new way of doing things is totally worthwhile. In that way, you've created a contagious chain of respect that will help things move much more smoothly at home.

FINAL THOUGHTS ON CHAPTER 3

Respect is a powerful topic and you are walking away from this chapter with a set of tools to start using ASAP. Don't forget, your actions carry a tremendous amount of weight, and your kids will follow in your footsteps even if it seems like they never listen or pay attention to you. Children are always watching, and the example you set, the things you model, will stick with your son or daughter. If you are able to work more respect into your daily routine, you'll help your child fill up his or her internal reservoir of confidence. Equipping your child with that tool is priceless. You will accomplish this by choosing your words wisely and making sure you communicate clearly. Be accurate and be honest. Do your best to interact with your child in a kind way because kindness matters. Talk to your child the same way you would like other people to talk to them, and the way you want them to talk to others. Then, hold them accountable for respectfully rewriting their own sassy or edgy statements. Big picture: These are life skills, not just parenting skills. Using and practicing these tools in all areas of your life will make it much easier to reach for them in the comfort of your own home.

CHAPTER 4

Set Limits:
Say yes, no, maybe so

Watch Video Message:
Dr. Stephanie O'Leary Introduces Chapter 4

http://www.stephanieoleary.com/intro-to-
chapter-4-of-parenting-in-the-real-world.html

The concept of setting limits is not foreign to you, because after all, you're a parent. You have undoubtedly been taking your best stab at setting limits for some time now. I have yet to meet a parent that has a complete aversion to limits, so there's no hard sell here. Are there differences as to where parents draw their lines in the sand? Absolutely. Is it sometimes hard to know when to push and when to back down? I'm sure! For now, let's start with the idea that limits and boundaries are things you will have to set up and navigate as a parent.

THE ERA OF INSTANT GRATIFICATION

I believe wholeheartedly that parental limit setting has gotten much harder in the last decade, and I suspect that trend will continue. This is based on the observation that our world is a virtual cornucopia of instant gratification. The net impact on your family of this fast paced, get-it-when-you-want-it society just might correlate with the presence of technology in your life and in your home. Before you read any further, I want to be clear. I'm not bashing technology and I'm not anti-technology. I'm using technology right now to put these thoughts on paper to share with you. I see that there are tremendous benefits and opportunities provided by technological advances and devices. I'm certainly not one to throw the baby out with the bathwater, but I am one to say, "Baby, it's time to get out of the bath for a little while. You're turning into a prune!"

When access to technology becomes pervasive, all of us, kids included, become accustomed to instant gratification. I experienced this first hand a few years ago and it was a huge wake-up call for me. One fateful day, my car's Bluetooth hookup broke, rendering me no longer able to stream music while driving. After spending my commute scanning the regular old radio dial that first day, I was overcome with nostalgia and intrigued by all that AM/FM had to offer. So, long story short, I never went back to the instamatic, auto-shuffle, personally selected playlist scenario, at least not by piping it through my Subaru's speakers. And let me tell you, that change hit my kids like a brick wall. Upon hearing a request from the backseat for a specific song, I had to explain to my kids that we could scan through the stations to see what was playing, but that we couldn't necessarily hear what we wanted, when we wanted it. We couldn't rewind, replay, or skip what came through on the radio waves.

My children looked at me like I had three heads. Well, one of them did. The other insistently instructed me on how to get his desired song to play from my phone, even without the Bluetooth (and I'm pretty sure his method would have worked, but I digress). In that instant I saw how both of my children expected instant gratification. It launched me into a walk down memory lane and they both gazed with disbelief as I recounted the hours I spent lying on the carpet in my room beside my boom box, patiently waiting to hear and record my favorite new song from the radio onto a cassette tape. Trust me, they might as well have been on an archaeological dig. This conversation played out like a History Channel exposé to them. After all, at that time my five-year-old son could GPS his way pretty much anywhere and my then eight-year-old daughter could voice dial any number of people in a snap using my phone. They were clearly used to getting what they wanted as soon as they wanted it.

I'm sure you have many examples of your own, times when your child could not tolerate a car ride without a DVD player, or could not sit at a table in a restaurant without an electronic device. Kids are used to fast-forwarding through commercials when watching shows. They can order, download, upload, or stream any number of videos, clips, or other forms of entertainment on demand. Children have instantaneous access to the entire database of the Internet, often in their back pocket. (And who knows more than Wikipedia?) In fact, they probably don't even have to type to get their questions answered. There's an app for that, right? If you need further evidence, or if you are curious to see just how reliant you and your family are on technology's instant gratification, gather everyone together on a regular old evening and cut your home's cable and wireless connections. Or hide the chargers for all the devices you own and see what unfolds over the next 48 hours. Potential Armageddon.

I'm not saying that we adults are any less prone to this phenomenon. Trust me, there are days when I feel the need to detox from my phone and unplug completely, but I do know that when today's adults were all budding little human beings, a lot of this technology did not exist.

Sure, there were televisions (even ones with remote controls), and telephones (some with cords), and some version of prehistoric video games, but you could only watch one station at a time, and there was no pause, fast-forward, or rewind option. There were no texts, but there were beepers (remember that!). Did we even have email? I think we may have had pen pals. See, even I can't recall clearly what life was like before smart phones. I do know that we had to use maps or ask for directions by interacting with other human beings, face to face. Some of the rest of it is a blur, but there were many more limits to cope with just by virtue of the fact that society had far less opportunity for instantaneous gratification. The funny part of this is, think of what our grandparents, or great-grandparents, or five generations back would say about how we were raised! Our ancestors may not hold a candle to us when it comes to the tech world, but I bet my bottom dollar that their ability to tolerate distress, wait patiently, and handle limits would far surpass anything that exists today.

So, what is all of this doing to our brains? I have no idea. I'm sure some scientists and researchers out there can tell you more about that, but I can weigh in on how this affects our kids and changes the rules for parents. This instant gratification thing deprives kids in very basic ways.

Children have far fewer opportunities to develop patience, and at the same time they have incredibly high expectations when it comes to getting their needs met. Most times, children are used to obtaining what they want quickly and easily, and if and when that is not possible, they struggle to cope. Having high expectations and low frustration tolerance probably won't work out too well in the real world where no one is catered to and consequences are real. The good news is, there are steps you can take to help your child strengthen coping skills and deal with limits and real-world frustrations.

DRAW THOSE LINES IN THE SAND

Your job as a parent in this current version of the real world is to make sure your kids can cope with limits. Certainly, some forces work against you here, so you will have to work harder and smarter to prepare your children for what's to come when they leave the nest (and hopefully help things go smoothly until they're ready to fly). See, down the road, when real-world things happen—like being pulled over by a police officer, facing peer pressure, hearing from a boss that they have to stay late even though they have concert tickets—there will be no pause button, no rewind option, and no time or space for a frustrated temper tantrum. The stakes at that point will also be much higher, so taking steps to prepare your child for the future of limits is important.

How do you do that? You set limits now. Chances are, you do this in some form or another already. From the very start you set limits with your kids. When they were small, it was about safety. You corralled your children into secured, baby-proofed spaces and repeatedly explained which things could or could not be touched, eaten, stuck in ears, etc. As your children grew a bit older, you probably started setting limits around sleep, nutrition, and general activities. You may have said things like, "Yes, it's time to get ready for bed," or, "No, you can't have ice cream right now."

Limits. Boundaries. These guidelines that help to create a well-thought-out environment for your child that's appropriate for her age and temperament. Notice we are talking about drawing lines in the sand here, not taking out the sharpie and marking up your hardwood floors. You will set limits based on the specifics of the situation at hand and you will continue to reevaluate these limits and alter them over time so they make sense for your family. This doesn't mean that they disappear when the wind blows or when your child pushes back. You won't cave in or abandon your expectations in a situation once you have set a limit, but what makes sense on Monday—with all the particulars of Monday—may not make sense on Saturday, or next month, or next year. In that case, you will redraw your line in the sand and set a new limit that makes sense for the current situation. This makes sense because the same limits that worked for your 18-month-old will not work for your teenager. Moreover, what might be appropriate and wildly successful for one child may not work for another, regardless of age or gender or anything else that seems like it might have good predictive power. Limits and boundaries are not one-size-fits-all, so let's spend some time breaking down exactly how to put them in place.

IT'S OKAY FOR YOUR CHILD NOT TO BE OKAY

Before we go any further with this topic, let's discuss how comfortable you are seeing your child in a distressed state. I would be doing you a disservice to gloss over the fact that limit setting may upset your child, and if you are not ready to deal with that, limit setting will likely backfire. You can be right there on the verge of implementing a well-thought-out boundary only to second-guess yourself at your child's first whimper. You know those things that pull on your heartstrings, the pretty pleases, the puppy-dog eyes, possibly pooling with tears. Don't forget the venomous sass that seems to zap you where you're raw, right in your most vulnerable spots. All of this feedback may cause you to question your intentions, waver in your conviction, and even doubt whether you are a good parent!

I'm not going to send you out there into the trenches of parenting unprepared, because I know the reality of a child's defenses, and they will do what all humans programmed for survival will do. Children will fight tooth and nail to have their needs met, and remember, your kid has big needs and big expectations. I know what you are up against because all the distress your child feels when you set a limit will be handed right back to you, and not on a silver platter (think food fight—and not plastic cutlery either).

Basically, you have to come to terms with the fact that your child will be upset when you set limits and create boundaries. Who wouldn't be? I would rather have what I want, when I want it than have to wait or see things from someone else's perspective. As a parent, you know that the waiting and seeing are part of life, so you march on to help your child prepare, and you do it with your eyes wide open to the fact that your kid may be sort of pissed off. I'm telling you this so it doesn't blind-side you, so you are not ambushed just when you started to feel you were on the right track.

Setting limits and creating boundaries means that your child might, or will, feel temporarily not okay (sad, mad, devastated, hysterical, despondent, silent, etc.). In the moment, you may not be able to see that the distress is temporary because your child's feelings will be big, loud, intense, and even explosive. I'm going to make it crystal clear. Your child will be temporarily not okay, and that's okay. It's okay for them to not be okay. This is part of the process. This is actually the most important part of limit setting because there are things out there in the real world that will cause your child distress in the future. Getting used to managing and handling uncomfortable feelings helps your child prepare for all that the real world will throw at them.

You are teaching your child to deal with—and tolerate—temporary discomfort and to delay his or her gratification for some good reason that's not currently clear, but that will eventually be recognized. Big picture, it's not about the outcome. Ten years from now it will not matter all that much if your child went to the mall or stayed home. It's not about getting that toy or not having it. It's not about watching the next show or heading to bed. All of those outcomes are relevant day to day, but when your child is

21, it's not the ride to the store, or the Lego set, or the TV episode that stays with him; it's how well he is able to tolerate distress, limits, and boundaries that will make a genuine difference in his quality of life.

Hold onto the fact that it is A-okay for the limits you set to upset your child. The next section of this chapter will help you make sure that the limits you choose are well-thought-out and that they match your intentions for the situation at hand. You have nothing to worry about there. You'll be ready for the distress—the temporary distress—that is for the greater good in the long run, and when you see it, you will keep in mind that it's all part of growing up. It's not about keeping your child happy every single instant of her life, but about giving her the tools to be a capable person who is able to find happiness out there in the real world.

If you feel like you need one final vote of confidence, especially if you know that it's hard for you to see your child upset, I'll mention just one more thing. Your child will come to terms with all of this at some point. Somewhere down the line, either at home with you or out there in the real world, his ability to tolerate distress and delay gratification will be tested. Please, please, please let him work through this with you, and do it as soon as possible. The older a child is when this happens, the harder they fall. Plus, the real world is full of unpredictability, and full of people who will not care about your child half as much as you do, even on your worst day! This is one lesson that your child will learn best while perched above the safety net of your unconditional love. So, when you hear that you are the meanest, worst parent in the world—when your child disowns you, slams the door, or cries so hard she looks like she is about to puke—pause and remind yourself that you are doing it right. Then, if it helps, you can even close your eyes and imagine relaxing at the beach, sitting right there next to your gorgeous line in the sand.

YES, NO, MAYBE SO

Now it's time to talk about limit setting made easy. Remember that you, as the parent, are ultimately in charge, like it or not. You are the grown-up and the call maker. That means that the first step to limit setting is to stop and think about how you want things to turn out based on whatever situation you are in. Your child asks you a question, presents a need, a wish, a demand, and you have to make a decision. Remember that your decision may not be the same on Monday as it is on Tuesday. Monday's situation is probably different from Tuesday's. That's okay; that's the real world.

Sometimes the things your child brings to you may not be a big deal at all. The requests you hear may be for things you don't mind allowing. Sometimes you may think it's cute you're even be asked at all. These boundaries are easy. These are yeses. When you say yes to your child, mean it. If there are ramifications or qualifiers, things you expect in order for that yes to happen, that's fine. In that case, you just have to be sure to communicate clearly and respectfully using "If-yes." "If-yes" is the modern day *maybe*. Basically, if you do this, that, or another thing, the answer is yes. Choose wisely here because once you commit to an answer, it sets a poor precedent to go back and change it. If you do not have the mental or physical wherewithal to follow through, stick with a plain and simple yes or a no. Here are some examples of plain and simple yeses and if-yeses:

Yes	If-Yes
Yes, you can watch a show for 20 minutes.	If you take a shower and brush your teeth by 8:30, you can watch a show for 20-minutes.
Yes, you can go to Logan's on Saturday.	If you text me Logan's parents' contact info, and show me that you've finished your English report tonight, then you can go to Logan's after dinner on Saturday.
Yes, you can order that Lego set.	If you choose one toy from your room that you don't really use and donate it today, then you can order a Lego set that's $20 or less.

Either option is fine, just think carefully about what you want and what you mean when you say yes to your child. If it's a plain and simple yes, with no contingencies, then you say yes and everyone moves on. If your yes involves an expectation for your child, something he needs to do to earn it, then use if-yes. Communicating honestly about your expectations will prevent you from feeling pushed or unappreciated down the road if your child starts stepping over your line in the sand. If your child does not accept or like the ifs that are attached to the yeses, that's fine. Remember, it's okay for him to be not okay. You made your expectations clear and you put some thought into them before you started, so in response to any grumblings you can say, "I gave you my answer; it's your choice now." There may be a "but Mom" or a "but Dad," presented in a whining, grating, or exasperated tone, but you can handle those. They will not move your line in the sand and you will not engage in a power struggle or debate because there's nothing to go back and forth about. You've thought it through and placed it in your child's hands. Now, you let it go.

In the end, it is your child's choice. You can tell your child, honestly, that you want her to have whatever she is asking for. Truly, you do, but then she will have to do her part. If not, it's okay. Don't shower by

8:30; you'll still have to shower but you just don't get the extra show. It's totally fine not to get Logan's parents' contact info; just know that you're choosing not to go to his house on Saturday. The Lego set? Take it or leave it—it's totally up to you.

Know that your child is learning a lot with these if-yeses. She is learning to navigate the real world, or the semi-real world of your family, and decide how much effort and energy she is willing to put toward gaining what she wants. The more you practice delivering these clear, well-thought-out if-yeses, the more your child practices coping with limits, and you put the ball in her court, which automatically empowers your child. If your child does not succeed or doesn't get what she wanted, it's a lot harder for the blame to be tossed back on you (even if your child may try). Plus, if and when your child does succeed, she will feel a sense of accomplishment in having worked for or toward something. The life skills just keep on coming. And all because of a well-thought-out if-yes.

On the other side of the coin, we have things that are clear nos. Naturally, this can be a bit more complicated and emotions may run higher. When your teen says, "Mom, can I get a dozen piercings tonight at Mary's? She knows how. It's safe, I promise!" Or, when your eight-year-old sticks her head into your shower to ask, "Can I make popcorn with oil on the stove? I just saw how on a cooking show and it's easy. I wanna do it right now." Or, when your middle schooler says, "Dad, Brad's older brother said he would take us out and let us practice driving his car in the lot behind the school. Can I?" I'm guessing that your ultimate goal in any one of these situations is to not let it happen. Thus, these situations are easy to call. I gave you the hell-no examples. However, there are a bunch of other times when you will carefully consider the time, place, and details, and the magic eight ball will still land on no. That will be your line in the sand, and that limit is okay.

Let's talk about how to get the message across and how to set a limit and say no like you mean it while minimizing the collateral damage. If you've read the earlier chapters, especially chapters 1 and 2, you are familiar with how to listen, pause, validate. Now is a perfect time to bust out those tools. If you've skipped around in the book, or started with this chapter, I'll review quickly. Your child comes to you with something she wants, something she feels strongly about. If you say no right out of the gate, things will likely escalate quickly. Instead, start by listening fully to what your child is asking for, and then take a second to prepare before you jump into validating her. Empathize a little, and let your child know that you see where she is coming from (even if you don't, even if what she is asking for is insane, poorly timed, and potentially illegal in certain states). Don't judge, lecture, or ridicule. Then, just before you set the limit, tell your child that you know it may be hard for her to hear your answer. This gets your child ready to hear you say no and mean it.

You'll do all of this calmly, empathically, and with as much respect as possible—all the while getting ready for whatever backlash is to come. Check out these nos, and see if they seem doable:

Child Asks/Begs:	Mom, can I get a dozen piercings tonight at Mary's? She knows how. It's safe, I promise!
Parent Sets a Limit:	That sounds like something you really want, and I know this is hard for you to hear. I'm not comfortable with you getting piercings at Mary's, the answer is no.
Child Asks:	Can I make popcorn with oil on the stove? I just saw how on a cooking show and it's easy. I'm gonna do it now.
Parent Sets a Limit:	That sounds awesome; maybe we can do that together. We can talk about it when I come downstairs. Please don't touch the stove without me.
Child Asks/Pleads:	Dad, Brad's older brother said he would take us out and let us practice driving his car in the lot behind the school. Can I?
Parent Sets a Limit:	That sounds like it would be really cool, so this may be hard for you to hear. I'm not comfortable with you driving before you have your permit. The answer is no.

I know that your child's shouting and resistance may come back at you before you even finish delivering your well planned no. So, how do you respond to the backlash? You wait it out. You don't have to respond at all until your child calms down. Dealing with your very own temporary discomfort here may be hard, and strategies like taking deep breaths, mentally distracting yourself from the onslaught (try counting backward from 100 by 3's, or naming an animal for every letter of the alphabet), or— my personal favorite—putting yourself in a time out, will help. Your child may also try to fight with you and pull you into a conflict. After all, that's a great tactic. When you feel like you're losing, dragging your opponent into the ring with you seems to make sense. That said, you, as the parent, know that this is not a competition. You cannot afford to engage in a battle of wills with your child because there are only two ways it can end, and neither is great. One is for you to give in. The other is for you to hurt your child—usually verbally or emotionally—to gain the upper hand. It's not good, and everyone loses. Your child loses because either they escape the limit you set and skip the life lesson or become the target of your anger. You lose because you either erase your line in the sand or hurt your child. The solution is don't fight. Don't take the bait. Stick to your no. Go back to your beach. Become one with your line in the sand.

FINAL THOUGHTS ON CHAPTER 4

Now you have learned the tools you need to say yes, if-yes (the modern day *maybe*), or no without getting into a battle with your child. Using the strategies from this chapter, most exchanges will end with a win-win, even if your child does not necessarily see or experience victory in the moment. Keep in mind that each time you set a limit for your child you provide an opportunity for him or her to learn to persevere, to delay gratification, and potentially earn something he or she desires. Remember to think carefully about what you want before you give an answer, and then deliver your yes, if-yes, or no calmly and clearly. Be ready for disappointment and tolerate temporary distress knowing full well it's part of the process. Not only will the practice of limit setting help your household run more smoothly, but it will ultimately bring you closer to your children—all the while teaching them how to cope with limits and preparing them for the day they will be responsible for setting limits on their own.

CHAPTER 5

Be Accountable:
How to say sorry and mean it

Watch Video Message:
Dr. Stephanie O'Leary Introduces Chapter 5

http://www.stephanieoleary.com/intro-to-chapter-5-of-parenting-in-the-real-world.html

As a parent, one of the most powerful things you can do is apologize to your kids—and mean it. This tool allows you to repair missteps, which, despite your best efforts, will happen—some days more than others! Even more impactful, though, when you deliver a sincere apology, you hold yourself accountable for your actions or inactions. You step up and own what you did or didn't do, what you said or didn't say, and how it all went down—including possible eye-rolls and shouts of exasperation. Your ability to own your stuff will never be lost on your child, no matter how old he or she is. Kids pay attention to parents—even when actively ignoring you. They pay attention enough to know what they're ignoring! Your child watches you all the time, particularly during the early years when just figuring out what the world is all about. You are constantly in the spotlight when it comes to your child. When you hold yourself accountable and demonstrate ownership, you model that same skill set for your child. You teach your child how to take responsibility while at the same time sending the message that it's a desirable thing to do.

Big picture, a great way to raise a child who is accountable and who takes ownership over their choices is to do those very same things yourself. One incredibly simple way to practice this is by delivering heartfelt—or at least well-thought-out—apologies.

SORRY!

It makes sense to start a chapter on apologies at the beginning—with "I'm sorry." Fair warning, I have strong opinions on this topic, which is probably why there's an entire chapter devoted to the art of apologizing in the first place. I think that the phrase "I'm sorry" is overused and overrated. If you ask either of my children what I dislike hearing more than anything else, I bet you anything they would say it's, "I'm sorry." When I hear those words, and when they are empty or said on reflex, my response is, "Don't tell me you're sorry; change your behavior," and I'm dead serious. Please don't get me wrong. I'm not a callous, jaded person who feels above it all. I screw up, and I experience remorse and regret just like everyone else, but those two words, "I'm sorry," are said and heard so often in our society that I wonder if they have any meaning left at all.

Think about all the times you say you're sorry throughout the day. You bump into someone—sorry. You unknowingly step into line ahead of someone—sorry. You drop something—sorry. Someone complains to you—sorry. We get it; you are sorry, sorry, sorry. In most cases, you're probably just trying to be polite—and for some reason, "I'm sorry" rolls off the tongue with more ease than excuse me. I have no idea why, but it may be a generational phenomenon because my grandparents were some of the most well-mannered people I've ever met and they didn't gain those points by being overly apologetic.

I also know that many times when parents say sorry they don't truly mean it. These instances are typically followed by the word "but," and then a whole bunch of other stuff that undoes any potential intended apology. Kids are trained, often forced, to say sorry from the time they are just learning to speak, and parents often feel forced to choke up those same words from time to time to smooth things over. I know it's a widely practiced custom, and perhaps even a skill that some parents seek to cultivate. Well, let me go on record—I'm not into it.

I'm so not into it that when my daughter was young I found myself having a guttural reaction to the playground/playgroup phenomena where mothers would make apologies on behalf of their babbling infants. It seemed insane to me, for a few reasons. Just a few months down the road, this pattern quickly evolved into an expectation for toddlers to say sorry for any number of "offenses." First of all, children, babies really, have no idea what the heck they're saying! Don't get me wrong, they are aware of a lot. You show an infant something blue, say, "blue" with a wide-eyed gaze and lovely high pitched voice, point to something else that's blue and, your little one probably started to understand what blue was all about. You cautiously allow your young child to feel heat, say, "hot," and you can practically see the brain cells firing and connecting. Young children get it, because it makes sense. Even love. We show our children love, give them love, and say, "I love you." Children experience this, internalize what those words mean, and, in an adorable mushy fashion, they knock your socks off when they use it to communicate their love for you. All of this makes sense.

So back to "I'm sorry." That statement didn't make sense to me when I was a young parent. I could not for the life of me understand how this "teaching moment" taught anything at all. From my perspective, this is how things looked on the baby playdate:

> Adorable baby, we'll call her Riley, plays with this cool thing—a round, bouncy, rolling thing that sometimes makes noise. It's a bright, awesome color. It's fun. Then another littler person crawls over and puts her hands on the round, bouncy, rolling thing and all of the sudden the cool thing is gone. Riley uses her hands to grab at it and get it back. She wants the fun, cool thing. This goes on and on, and now the other littler person is crying, but Riley has the fun thing and scoots away so she can enjoy it.

We've all seen this play out, right? Heck, we've all been there (insert job, mate, car for the ball and the real world just entered stage left), but is Riley sorry? No, I don't think she is. I think Riley is happy to have what she wanted, and I appreciate that. If someone put his or her hands on my job, or mate, or car, I would probably react with the grown-up version of Riley's attack plan. In some ways, not much has changed.

Now, back to the playdate. Riley isn't being reared *Lord of the Flies* style, so her mom swoops in and says something along the lines of, "Riley, that's not nice. Say sorry. Riley's sorry." All of this is probably delivered while swiping the ball from Riley and giving it to the other child. You see, the problem here is that Riley is not learning that "I'm sorry" is a genuine apology. She's learning that it's something you're forced to say when you feel upset, and even when you do, you still stay upset. The interesting part of this entire dynamic is that when adults hear "I'm sorry," they assume the child knows what it means. Adults, parents included, interpret those words as if they have intention. Eventually, kids start to use "I'm sorry" to clean up all sorts of missteps and poor choices, all the while never grasping the true meaning of an apology. To me that feels a little bit crazy making, and I'm not sorry to say so.

MAKE A BETTER CHOICE NEXT TIME

What is the solution to this mind-baffling quandary? My vote is to put the kibosh on the empty, "I'm sorry" as early as possible. As a parent, I decided to take the bull by its horns and come up with a tool to teach my kids accountability and ownership—the values I am most interested in instilling. That's when, "I'll make a better choice next time" was born. I'm not sure exactly how it came to fruition, likely through trial and error, but it made sense. By the time my daughter was a toddler, our household apology protocol when something like this: Apologize for what happened, then say I'll try to make a better choice next time. For example, "I'm sorry I opened your lotion and dumped it all over the counter. I'll make a better choice next time." Or, "I was mad and I hit Rachel. I'm sorry, I'll make a better

choice next time." Or, "I climbed the bookcase and the music box fell. I'm

sorry it broke. I'll make a better choice next time."

In my book (no pun intended), an apology—a genuine reflection of

accountability and ownership—starts with identifying and saying what

went wrong and then vowing to make a better choice next time. "I'm

sorry" didn't necessarily cover these bases because lots of times kids, and

grown-ups for that matter, may have to take ownership and apologize for

things they are not really all that sorry about. If the entire communication

is hinged on someone simply being sorry, the point is lost. There's no real

motivation or expectation to change your behavior in the future.

Will kids change their behavior simply to avoid having to say sorry

in the future? I don't think so because uttering two words does not lead to

true accountability. Plus, when saying "I'm sorry" acts as a little magic

eraser, things can backfire completely. The habitual use of "I'm sorry" can

perpetuate poor choices being repeated as kids learn they just have to say

the right words and then move on without skipping a beat. I know I'm

simplifying. I know that there are real consequences in life and that,

eventually, friends, teachers, classmates, teammates, etc., will catch on and treat a habitual empty apologizer differently, but that time comes way down the road. I would rather not start down that road to begin with.

When you start practicing these new, genuine, well-thought-out apologies, saying "I'll make a better choice next time" provides an opportunity to have a real conversation about next time. Your child says they will try to do something different in the future and thus you have a lovely invitation to discuss what that might be, how it might look, and what they might try. You can even ask your son or daughter how he or she plans to do that different thing or make that different choice. If you can partner with your child rather than accuse and judge them, you will have an opportunity to help them figure things out and chart a new course. Even better, the first part of a genuine apology is all about ownership, so you will be helping your child pinpoint what in the world they are apologizing for in the first place.

All of this takes practice. You'll spend time helping your child identify exactly what he did—or didn't do. You'll help your child find the words to express his missteps. At the playdate, you will have to explain things. Maybe you will say, "Someone else also wanted to play with the ball because it's so cool. I know that's hard. Let's see if we can play together or take turns." Then you can spend time teaching your child how to play and share (and sharing is hard!), rather than exhausting your efforts on trite apology lessons. Using this approach means being honest with your child, and down the road your child will be able to communicate honestly as well. Maybe you will hear things like, "She wanted a turn but I didn't want to share so I hit her. I'm sorry. I'll make a better choice next time." That statement, while brutally honest, is exactly what happened from the child's perspective. Is it nice and neat like "I'm sorry"? Nope. It's gritty, and sometimes messy, but it's real, and I'm sure you expect nothing less since we're doing this parenting thing in the real world. Ownership, accountability, and a vow to try better next time.

WHOSE IDEA WAS THIS ANYWAY?

Clearly, I stand by my convictions and feel certain that saying what happened and committing to make a better choice next time is an excellent way to deliver a sincere apology. Ownership and accountability are wonderful traits, and the more you and your child practice them the better. Plus, a vow to try and do things better in the future sounds fantastic. This last part is particularly powerful, and deserves a little more explanation.

I mentioned before that parents sometimes think that making a child apologize will deter them from doing the same thing again. The thought is, apologizing is uncomfortable, so if you don't mess up again, you won't have to apologize again. That sounds like a great line of reasoning, but as I said before, I rarely see it work that way. Moreover, the real world is full of natural consequences that will show up even after the words "I'm sorry" are uttered. At a certain point, there will not be a parental figure on the sidelines providing a clue that reminds your child to pay attention to their choices. As a parent, you can prepare your child by helping them think about apologizing from the inside out, as soon as possible.

Having your child take accountability by saying they will make a better choice next time accomplishes this goal. You see, people, kids included, like to be right. Our brains like it when we think something will happen and then it does. This desire to be correct shapes our perspective, and you can capitalize on this facet of human nature by using it to help your child mature into a responsible, confident adult. If along the way it helps take down the intensity at home, so be it!

Keeping in mind that everyone wants to be right, when you teach your child to say "I'll make a better choice next time," he automatically becomes invested in the accuracy of that statement. Your child will buy into the idea of making a better choice next time simply because he said it, and he likes to be right.

Another point to keep in mind—words matter. The aim is not to have your child say, "I'll never do it again, I promise!" That's not practical. That statement is highly improbable and potentially impossible to deliver on. In fact, it's so unlikely to be true that your child probably won't even believe it as she's saying it. Kids are smart that way, but "I'll make a better choice next time" will give your son or daughter something to grab onto. There is acknowledgement that a choice is being made, and a choice is something your child can influence. Better yet, your child is committing to try, not to be perfect or to do it just right, but to improve upon their prior actions and choices—and that's completely doable. Your child walks away from the situation feeling that she has a choice and can make it a better one in the future. She will believe this is possible. In one fell swoop, this tool allows you to successfully avoid empty, meaningless sorrys, and also equips your child with a life skill that allows her to be accountable and prove herself right as she strives to do better. If that's not self-perpetuating motivation, I'm not sure what is.

PRACTICE WHAT YOU TEACH

This chapter began with a plea for you to take accountability and deliver heart-felt, genuine apologies to your child(ren), and all I've been doing is talking about how to teach your child how to say sorry—or not—while really meaning it. That was on purpose, and I'll tell you why. I have found time and again that parents, myself included, are most attentive when listening to things they can do for their children. This setup puts you—the parent—back in the comfortable role of teacher and guide, and you tend to soak up information confidently and objectively from that perspective. I took advantage of this when deciding how to best communicate these critical points about apologizing and ownership, and I made the first part of this chapter all about your child(ren).

Alas, the cruise through the comfort zone has ended and it's time to get serious. Let's talk about using this new tool in your parenting practice. Don't write this part off just because you don't like the spotlight shining on you. I know the light is bright, but you can totally handle this, I promise. Plus, it will be over soon and the payoff is huge.

As a parent, how do you feel about apologizing? Do you say sorry a lot? Are you practically allergic to it? Maybe you fall somewhere in between. When a parent, or anyone for that matter, lets sorry roll off their lips quite readily, probably without thinking, and often without intention, those apologies reach your child's brain and sound something like the *whan-whan-whan* of the Charlie Brown teacher. If the apology is delivered in a tone—or at a volume—that triggers your child's proverbial fingers to be inserted far into his ears, your sentiments are totally blocked out. This is not to suggest that you don't offer sincere apologies to your child, I'm just asking you to take stock and see if there's any white noise going on as well.

Some parents are not at all comfortable with the idea of apologizing. This pattern may arise for any number of reasons, and I'm going to go out on a limb here and guess that parents in this group rarely, if ever, heard a sincere apology from their own caregivers. In fact, my gut says that people in this camp were taught that apologizing signifies some sort of weakness. It might feel like losing, admitting defeat, or being flat-out wrong. An apology may even fall in the category of things to be ashamed of—things to avoid at all costs. Maybe parents who have developed an apology allergy are just sick and tired of feeling forced into uttering meaningless sorrys. In response, it's possible that anti-apologizers are taking a hard line by not saying sorry at all. Regardless of the root cause, taking a risk and using the tool of apologizing in a genuine fashion will have a tremendous impact on your relationship with your child.

NO BUTS ABOUT IT

For all parents, there is one brilliant way to spoil an apology—even a trite little "I'm sorry." It's the word "but." Think of it this way; if you put "but" after an apology, you may as well erase what you said in the first place. "But" is sneaky like that. It discredits anything you might have shared or intended, and shifts 100 percent of the focus to what's coming next. Here are some more examples to illustrate the negating power of "but":

"But" Statement	What Your Child Hears
I'm really sorry I yelled, but you are being so stubborn right now and you are not listening!	I am the problem.
I know I shouldn't have talked about that in front of your friends, but you were being really pushy and you just wouldn't let it go!	It's my fault that mom embarrassed me.
I'm sorry you can't go to the mall like we planned, but your brother has extra homework and we just don't have time.	My dad cares more about my brother than he does about me.

"But" is not going to help you make your points here. You'll have to go back to biting the inside of your cheek if you feel a "but" creeping up anywhere in the vicinity of your apology. Remember, there is no "but" in an apology, and there is a period at the end of an apology—plain and simple. Try these rewrites on for size and see if you can envision yourself saying them:

Real Apology #1:	I completely lost my temper when I yelled before. That's not okay and I'm going to make a better choice next time.
What Your Child Hears:	Mom was pissed, and she's going to try not to lose it next time.
Going Deeper:	Mom messes up sometimes, cops to it, and tries to fix things. I wonder if there's something I can do differently too.
Even Deeper:	It's really not okay when people treat me badly, no matter how much they love me. I should try to treat the people I love well.
Real Apology #2:	Even though I felt frustrated when you kept pushing the issue with your friends here, it was not okay for me to talk like that. I'm going to make a point not to do that again.
What Your Child Hears:	Mom was really upset, but she gets it and she's going to try not to talk like that in front of my friends anymore.
Going Deeper:	Mom messes up sometimes, cops to it, and tries to repair things. Wonder if there's something I can repair too.

Even Deeper: It's really not okay when people treat me
                          badly, no matter how much they love me. I
                          should try to treat the people I love well.

Real Apology #3:   Honey, I know you were looking forward to
                          the mall and I know it won't help to hear
                          me say that I'm sorry plans have changed.
                          We can go tomorrow if you want.

What Your Child Hears: This is SO UNFAIR, and Dad sort of gets it.

Going Deeper: Things happen sometimes that are beyond
                          our control and my dad cops to it and tries
                          to make it better.

Even Deeper: I'm sort of lucky to have a dad who tries
                          hard to support me. I should make sure I
                          do my best to support the people I care
                          about.

That's better, right? Is it perfect? No way! We're not aiming for perfect; we're aiming for better. Now it's time to dive in and practice what you are teaching your child when it comes to being accountable and committing to do better in the future. If you are someone who says I'm sorry on repeat, bite your cheek and stop to think about what you really want to say. If you are someone who would rather stick a pencil in your eye than apologize, brace yourself because things are about to get real. Everyone is going to have to float a bit—or several miles—out of his or her comfort zone, but we're all in it together. Hop in the boat and start paddling.

FINAL THOUGHTS ON CHAPTER 5

Remember that the key to a true apology is holding yourself accountable for your stuff. If you felt pissed, say you felt pissed. If you felt tired, sad, scared, whatever, own it. Say it. And then say what you did that you know wasn't so great. No excuses. No blaming. Just being honest and holding yourself accountable. Let's be clear, your child does not make you do anything. There is nothing he or she can say, do, or be that makes you respond in a way you are not proud of. Can your child's actions or inactions contribute? Heck yeah, but don't give your power away; own what you do so you can do it differently in the future.

The sooner you start practicing, the sooner you will see shifts in your child and your family when it comes to personal responsibility. The blame game will have fewer players and there will be fewer rounds played. Finger pointing will be a thing of the past and you may even see more helping hands than you had back before you started holding yourself to the same high standards you want your kids to attain.

Teach your kids to take ownership and apologize sincerely by trying to do better in the future. Guide them by example. Give your child the gift of your own sincere apology when it's appropriate and drop the rest of the useless, meaningless, empty "I'm sorrys" like the dead weight they are. There's no room for that crap in the parenting boat; it's hard enough to stay afloat as it is. Your parenting detail at this point is to own your stuff so you can change your behavior. Trust me, your kids will follow suit. This is powerful stuff—buckle up, and make a better choice next time.

CHAPTER 6

Find Joy:
Loving and liking your child

Watch Video Message:
Dr. Stephanie O'Leary Introduces Chapter 6

http://www.stephanieoleary.com/intro-to-chapter-6-of-parenting-in-the-real-world.html

Joyful parenting sounds lovely, doesn't it? It takes me back to the days when my kids were infants. More specifically, when they were peacefully sleeping infants with rosy cheeks wearing adorable, clean PJs, or perhaps taking their first toddling steps. Everything was new and my babies were nothing short of precious. Trust me though—I don't have complete amnesia. I did not sleep through the night for seven years and often those cute PJs were decorated with anything from dog hair to remnants from a snack—yesterday's snack. That said, it does seem that babies are natural-born joy machines. Even with colic, teething, and overnight crying jags, big baby eyes and sweet baby smells—at least most of the time—are enrapturing. It's hard not to fall in love with your baby.

In reality, infants come into this world hardwired with magical abilities. Those big eyes and cute sounds I mentioned pull at our heartstrings by activating brain areas associated with nurturance. It's a fact; babies cast cuteness spells that urge moms and dads to provide love, care, and safety. What happens as your adorable infant grows up? He or she is still the apple of your eye, but the mushy, gushy, delicious emotion grows weaker. At times it may be absent. Think about it—when was the last time your made googly eyes at your son when he burped or hiccupped or laughed and playfully called your daughter a "stinker" when she passed gas? It's not cute anymore.

Plus, as children develop their own ideas—and the legs and voice to act on them—things shift even more. Children have more independence and can do more without your help. I will never forget the joy I felt when my kids first became able scrounge a cheese stick from the fridge or pull up their own pants. To a parent, those small acts are akin to winning the lottery—or at least a big-ticket scratch off. The flip side to this newfound I-can-do-it-myself attitude? More conflicts arise as "little" opinions, wants, and needs compete to be heard. Add this dynamic to a life already full to the brim with errands, lessons, deadlines, meals, and carpools and things can look bleak. Where did the joy go? What happened to those adorable sleeping babies?

You can quickly find yourself in a parenting slump when all of this real-world stuff hits at once. When I experience one of those desperate parenting days—or weeks—I think about my early days of parenthood. I remember the joyful moments when I felt love way down to my bones just from seeing my daughter's little smiling eyes light up or hearing my son sing when he didn't know I was listening. I dig deep and hold onto that connection. I remind myself that that is the same voice I hear now and those are the same eyes I look into today—even while my daughter zaps me with a death stare and my son asks, for the nineteenth time, if he can go on Brain-Pop.

A JOYFUL HOME

How do you rediscover joy in parenting amidst the day-to-day nonsense, and get back to liking your child as much as you love him? If you've read the previous chapters, you already have a set of go-to strategies for turning the volume up on things that invite joy back into your household. Up the respect factor, insert kindness, use accurate communication, listen, validate, offer sincere apologies to help clean up any mess ups, and provide well-thought-out limits and boundaries. These tools move you and your child(ren) toward less drama and fewer conflicts.

As you practice using these tools, the old stuff—conflict, screaming, yelling, threatening, meanness, endlessly repeating fights that never resolve themselves, guilt, dismissiveness, and countless other not-so-productive habits and interactions—will move out or be considerably downsized. That will leave empty space. It's the same phenomenon that occurs after a massive spring cleaning. You tidy up the closets, donate what you don't need or use, and suddenly have more room than you thought possible. You've just done this with your parenting relationship, so what do you want to fill all the newfound space with?

Remember, you are the parent, so you get to decide how to redecorate this emotional square footage that just showed up. Not to pressure you, but let's devote some brainpower and intention here before that old stuff moves back in!

Try this quick exercise. Think about what a joyful household means to you. What happens in a joyful household? What's said? What's seen? What's heard? How does your joyful household smell? Who's there? What fills the space in your joyful home? Try to connect with the things, interactions, and experiences that exist in your most joyful home.

If this task was a breeze—fantastic; if it feels like pulling teeth—don't give up. You've come this far, so give yourself a few days to be mindful of what joy means to you. Then, as you go through your day, make note of what pops into your head—the things you notice—the glimmers of joy you see and want more of, and the spaces and relationships that seem empty and in need of sprucing up. It's mindful, joyful redecorating, and it's much less expensive than the literal counterpart—and more valuable for your family.

Having a clear idea of what you want more of in your household will help you invite it in, so make a list of joyful intentions and get ready to be a joy magnet. Jot down three things that represent joy within your home. Then, keep the list in sight so you can read it on a daily basis. You can email it to yourself and leave it in your inbox to read each morning, or print it out and stick it on your bathroom mirror. Your list may include things like eating together, road trips, walking the dog, one-on-one time with kids, laughing, or being outside. Only you know what brings joy to you and your family. You are the expert in this department, so trust that whatever comes to mind, and know that it will serve you and your family well.

If you want more inspiration, visit www.StephanieOLeary.com and download the Quick Guide to a Joyful Home exercise using the following link (http://bit.ly/2dPrmsv) or simply scan the QR Code:

I mentioned earlier that I experience my own parenting slumps. I created my own list of joyful intentions to help keep things moving in a positive direction. In my house, music brings joy. Both of my children love music—making music, hearing music, and anything in between. I know that when there is music in the air, my children are joyful and, for some reason, I'm able to readily access that joy. My husband is the best when it comes to providing a soundtrack for our daily lives. When he pops on Pandora, the effect is instantaneous. My kids literally show up—wandering into the living room from whatever corner of the house they were in. I, on the other hand, am not as naturally thoughtful in this department. I have to remind myself to turn the music on, or up, because I'm more apt to get sidetracked by the doing and shuffling of the daily grind. In reality, it takes seconds to turn the radio on. I make a point to do it because all the other doing and shuffling is much easier to manage when it's set to music.

Another thing on my list of joyful intentions is laughter. Hearing kids laugh is crazy good, right? It starts with toddlers laughing so hard that milk sprays out their noses. Later, hearing a full body cackle or slaphappy, giddy laugh attack is still infectious. Plus, kids can be exceptionally funny—if and when you let them. Laughter is great. Laughter leads to joy in our household, so I have to remind myself to let my kids be funny sometimes while keeping my own sense of humor. Even when it seems like there is no time for silliness and wit—there is, I just have to take it. Things get done faster after a laugh anyway.

The third big item on my list of joyful intentions is holidays. I have the biggies covered in this department. Thanksgiving and Christmas are well-established, festive events full of tradition, and I am a kid at heart when it comes to planning and enjoying those seasons. My children share in that joy, but I have to remind myself to make space for their excitement on the little holidays that don't mean so much to me but are special to them. I make a conscious effort to let my children be creative and to relish in the magic of holidays, creating more joyful memories. Is it always convenient? No. Does bring joy to my home? You bet. Again, it's about stopping to take the time, disconnecting from the minutia, and appreciating the shamrock window decals or scraping through the craft store to find fake cobwebs—all the while praying the dogs don't choke on them.

Working to invite joyful events, experiences, and interactions into your home takes time, but it's a surefire way to create more of the positive emotions you experienced back when your child was programmed by Mother Nature to press all the right buttons and get you gushing. Focus on your list of joyful intentions, then sit back and see what happens. Know that joy comes in waves. Soak them up as they pass through. Cherish each moment. Remember that these fleeting, magical instances are not in competition with anything. Make space for them. They cannot be undone or stripped away, but they will end—and that's okay. Just savor the joy you experience. Be present when it shows up. You have all this extra space in your home now. Make a point to invite joy as a regular guest.

FALLING IN LOVE WITH YOUR CHILDREN—EVEN ON THE DAYS YOU MIGHT NOT LIKE THEM

Just before I got married, someone gave me a piece of advice that really stuck. A dear family friend said, "Wake up every morning and decide to love your husband. Decide to be in love with him, to stay in love with him, and to fall in love with him again and again. If things ever get off track, come back to this."

I am a practical person, so this sage guidance did not seem unromantic or trivial to me. It seemed powerful—and it made a lot of sense. Now, over a decade into this motherhood gig, I'm convinced it applies to parent-child relationships, too. Those connections require the same nurturance and tending as other partnerships, and because the footing is not equal, you—the parent—have to put in more work and effort. Keep in mind; this is always the case in parent-child relationships. Even when your child is grown up, you will forever be the parent and she will forever be the child. Some natural shifts toward reciprocal exchanges will take place, but you will give more and expect less. That's parenthood.

If you're ready to improve your relationship with your child—to like your child as much as you love him or her—it's time to take a stroll down memory lane. This journey will help you think about and purposely connect with your son or daughter. If you have more than one child, do this exercise separately, from start to finish, for each. Otherwise, your feelings may get all mixed up, and I'm not looking to send you into an emotional tailspin! This doesn't have to be time or labor intensive, and should take no more than ten minutes if you use the audio file located in the appendix at the end of this book (QR Code A: Walk Down Memory Lane). This recording leads you, step-by-step, through the exercise. The only other thing you will need is a piece of paper and something to write with. Tissues are optional. I'm not a crier, but reflecting on my own children often leaves me sentimentally reaching for a Kleenex.

The guided meditation starts by asking you to recall when and how you found out you were an expectant parent. Tell this tale accurately—don't edit—it's just you and your memories here. After you've relived that chapter, you'll move on to your child's birth story. Remember, no editing. The emotions may be intense—some positive, some negative, and all are welcome. You'll step back to view those first cries, first nights, first everythings, as you think about your baby growing up. You'll hold onto memorable moments from each stage of development—watching your tiny infant mature before your eyes. The memories that jump out may be significant events such as holidays, birthdays or vacations, or they may be the simplest of things—a mannerism that stuck in your mind, a precocious question, a car-ride conversation that stuck with you. This walk down memory lane is not about rehashing things or examining what you could have done differently. Aim for the feel of viewing home movies in your mind. You're just observing what happened—not judging or intervening—just seeing and remembering.

When you've completed your walk down memory lane, the next step is to find your paper and pen and write a list of all the things you love about your child. Don't think too hard—just write from your heart. Write what you feel now. Write about the little loves that have not been center stage in your mind for a long time, the sparks and pangs you remembered when you were looking back over your child's life. Basically, pour your heart out. The Kleenex are there if you need them.

When you're done, take a breather if you need to, because you are about to take another walk, only in the opposite direction. This journey will help you put things in perspective—to appreciate how precious time is and how fast life moves. Keep your pen and paper handy and find the recorded version of this exercise (QR Code B: Into the Future) in the appendix. This guided exercise will first ask you to think of your child as he or she is right now. Then, you'll skip forward in time several years and notice what's the same, and what has changed. Once you've had a good look, you'll flash forward a few more years and take stock of your child maturing in the years to come. You will keep going until you see your child as an adult. You'll think of all of the potential, the possibilities, and the challenges he or she might face. When you're ready, find your quiet space again and start the recording (QR Code B: Into the Future) for an opportunity to soak in a futuristic image of your son or daughter.

Now find your pen and paper, because it's time to make another list. Jot down all the things you hope the grown-up version of your child knows about himself—all the things you have taught him. The things you want him to hang onto as facts, the messages you pray he has swallowed whole and will tap into during his own journey. Write down what you want your child to know—to accept without a shadow of a doubt—about himself.

In short, make a list of all the things you want your child to pack up and take with him as he ventures into the real world one day. Things like:

You are better than good enough.

You are loved.

You're freakin' hysterical.

You are deserving.

You make the best pancakes in the world.

You're the best kind of goofball possible.

You are capable of amazing things.

You are strong.

You're never alone.

You're special.

This is not at all an exercise in charting your child's three-, five-, ten-, or twenty-year plan. It's a tool that provides perspective. This purposeful, futuristic thinking will help you connect with the fleeting nature of parenthood. Each week, each day, even each hour may seem long and painstaking sometimes, but in the big picture, the time you have with your child—with him under your roof and in your arms—is a tiny fraction of his journey. You have your child for a relatively short period of time. As a parent, it's important to take stock of that time and hone in on the messages you want your child to carry along to the real world upon leaving the nest. Time is not necessarily on your side here, and your mission— should you choose to accept it—is to solidify these loving messages while making sure no unnecessary baggage gets smuggled through parental security.

This chapter began with the intention of helping you fall in love with your child all over again—even during those times when you might not like her very much. I'm not sure if you used the Kleenex—or if you had a lot of these emotions sorted out and fresh in the front of your mind to begin with. Either way, reflecting on the past and glimpsing into the possibility of the future helps refocus on the here and now. You, as a parent, can act on this new perspective by making a point to read the lists you made, the parental love letters you've written, every day for the next three weeks. Twenty-one days, to be exact. This is enough time to make sure those loving messages sink in and become ingrained in your mind so you can make day-to-day decisions that reflect this love. Even when your child's amazing traits—the ones you gushed over just a few paragraphs ago—don't seem to be showing up, you'll be more apt to remember they're still there underneath the mood swings, temper tantrums, and eye rolls. This will help you see your child's amazing qualities clearly when they do make an appearance, however fleeting that cameo may be.

Having a daily reminder of the lessons and messages you want to share with your child will also keep you on point. Let's face it, life is busy and it is all too easy to get bogged down in the small, unimportant stuff like lunch money, dirty fingernails, and math tests. Losing sight of long-term priorities and the big picture of parenting is common. So every morning, for three weeks, review the loving messages you want your child to internalize and accept as facts of life. As all of us like to be right, you'll jump on every opportunity to communicate love to your child and start to see the best of her despite the insanity that may be brewing in the moment. You may even consider reading the lists to your child. Depending on her age, she may eat it up, act like you're crazy, or get a little defensive and pushy, but she will hear it. Then, when you send her those messages or love her as she deserves to be loved, she will notice—and that's the whole idea after all.

FINAL THOUGHTS ON CHAPTER 6

As you ventured forward to see your child in adulthood, were you struck by the notion that your child will be all grown up one day? He will get to make all of his own choices, including whether or not he will come home for Thanksgiving. He may even—one day far, far down the road—be making decisions for you. These things rarely cross your mind at 8 p.m. on a Tuesday when dinner is burning and homework is not yet started, or at 1:30 a.m. on Sunday when curfew is blown and kids are MIA, but the real world does not stop the game clock for time outs or penalties. Time keeps ticking, so it's important to hold onto your newly refreshed perspective and make a point to actively love your child.

I talk to parents all the time who are wrought with guilt about the choices they have made or the actions they have taken. This journey through time is the best tool I can offer to steer your parenting in a more genuinely loving direction. You'll get there by using daily reminders and a true commitment to seeing the best in your child, by loving your child unconditionally—even when he is not showing up as the best version of himself. This is a foundational cornerstone of *Parenting in the Real World*, and if you can devote time and energy here, the payoff will be tremendous for you and your child. There is a ton of joy there waiting to be discovered.

CHAPTER 7

Self Care for Parents:
The most important chapter,
even if you don't want to hear it!

Watch Video Message:
Dr. Stephanie O'Leary Introduces Chapter 7

http://www.stephanieoleary.com/intro-to-
chapter-7-of-parenting-in-the-real-world.html

PUT YOUR MASK ON

Self-care is a crucial part of being the best parent you can be. You are probably aware of this on some level, but you may well put taking care of yourself on the back burner because it's easier to reach for a tool or strategy to help your child than to reach for a tool to help yourself. Beyond that, self-care is not necessarily catchy or in vogue. It's easy to avoid, which means you sometimes go without while denying you need anything in the first place. Eventually, families will feel the impact of parents being spread too thin. Juggling the impossible while wearing a happy mask can only go on for so long before things start to fall apart behind the scenes.

I hope to shed some light on this topic and shift your expectations, since parenting is an incredibly demanding job that requires you to be at your best as often as possible. With a newfound understanding of how important it is to care for yourself so you can care for your child, I'm confident you can overcome any hang-ups and get out of your own way to become a balanced, thriving parent—with balanced, thriving children.

If you have read the previous chapters, you have a handful of go-to strategies to use at home every day. Maybe some are already helping you create a positive shift in your parenting practice. But if you feel stressed, depleted, irritable, frustrated, saddened, hopeless, confused, etc., it's challenging to implement even the most straightforward parenting strategy or approach. Plus, kids are creatures of habit. When you introduce a new idea, children push back because they want things to stay the same. The further off course things are, the more resistance you can expect as you try to make changes in the way you parent. If you are already down for the count—emotionally or physically—how can you bring your A-game to the playing field and start swinging with your new *Parenting in the Real World* tools?

Well, you can't. I know it would be a lot easier if all of the focus stayed on your child and the ways you can get him to do more of the things you want him to do. If I hopped on that bandwagon, tempting as it may be, it would only be a temporary fix and you would wind up back where you started in no time at all—just more exhausted and frustrated. Plus, I know that parents have only the best intentions—to raise children who are respectful, independent, and happy; to teach kids to handle frustrations and setbacks; and to appreciate accomplishments. Parents want children to successfully adapt to changes, express emotions, and work productively to get their needs met. These intentions are amazing, worthwhile, and absolutely doable, but—because there always seems to be a but—you have to be available to coach your child through this process. The easiest way to do this is for you—the parent—to live and breathe these very same ideals. You can help your child become adaptable and work toward having his needs met by modeling those life skills yourself.

I'm happy to report that you totally get to double-dip here. As I mentioned, by making changes and focusing on self-care you are modeling and teaching your child how to adapt and get her needs met. As a bonus, you actually get some of your needs met. I'm okay with parental self-care simply being about you getting your needs met—that's valuable. It was valuable before you had kids and will continue to be valuable every day for the rest of your life. However, in my experience, encouraging parents to take care of themselves simply because they deserve to is often not well received. Since I'm committed to keeping things practical and easy to use, for now, know that by helping yourself you are not only teaching your child how to prioritize his own self-care, but you are improving your ability to function as a parent. Double-dip. Win-win!

Here is a real world example to put things in perspective. Think about being on an airplane. Imagine everyone cramming in, eager to get to wherever the flight is heading. The airline attendants are explaining the safety procedures, including the familiar set of instructions pertaining to the oxygen masks.

This speech means something much different before children than it does when you have an infant in your lap. I will never forget the first flight I took as a new mother. My daughter was just six weeks old and I was flying from Atlanta to New York City to visit my parents. By an act of God, I made it to the seat while lugging the baby bag, floppy seat cover, pacifiers, burp cloths, and my own ID. I felt incredibly relieved to be buckling in and on my way. Then the flight attendant said something along the lines of, "By the way, if things get real and these masks fall into your face, go ahead and put yours on first while your helpless infant hangs out in your lap." I remember thinking, "No way in hell am I putting myself before my baby!" I even looked around, seeking validation from other horrified mothers only to find the majority of passengers zoned out and already reading their books or drifting off to sleep.

As a brand new parent, I had no idea what was in store for me. I had no idea how important and symbolic that oxygen mask was, or that a tuned-in parent puts the mask on first because it is the wise thing to do. You need to breathe—and function—because your child needs you. You put your mask on first. Is it easy? No. Is it the best option? Yes. Thankfully, I've never had to make that choice at 30,000 feet above sea level, but now, ten years later, I am intimately familiar with what happens if my mask is not securely fashioned—if my basic needs are not met while I'm trying to parent.

I do understand that we are not on a plane. In reality, it would be easier if we were—things are cut and dry while you're coasting thousands of miles above the ocean. Mask falls, put it on, help your kids. There may be a twinge of guilt, but when the stakes are high instincts take over.

No, you are not on a plane—you are parenting in the real world. You are prepping in the kitchen, shopping in the grocery store, working at your desk, chauffeuring in the driver's seat, and cheering in the stands. You are in the real world, doing what needs to be done day in and day out. Sometimes it's great—even extraordinary, but mostly it's routine, and perhaps it borders on monotonous. It's easy to get swept away in the routine and hard to know when you need oxygen. After all, there is no mask that dangles from your ceiling when you're beginning to falter. There are no alarms that buzz when your "cabin pressure" drops. No one will tell you that you need a break, a rest, a breath, and no one is giving you a speech each morning citing the critical importance of taking care of yourself before helping your kids.

I rarely tell people what to do. I do offer suggestions on how to try things a different way and then decide what works best. As a therapist, I help clients gather information and consider all sources objectively in order to make a plan or choice. It's actually a fundamental guideline of clinical ethics (so fancy!) to foster autonomy by creating the conditions necessary to make an informed choice. Basically, my job is not to boss anyone around, but I'm breaking this rule here. I'm telling you what to do. As a parent, you have to remember to put your mask on. Put your mask on.

FLIGHT PLAN FOR SELF-CARE

First things first, you have to figure out what you need. Maybe you can rattle off a list of your needs without skipping a beat, or maybe you have been so selfless in your role as a parent that you've lost perspective. Many parents come into my office saying, "I just need my child to be okay. That's all I need." Unfortunately, it's never that simple because you are the chicken that hatched that egg. The more balanced, healthy, and cared for you are, the better your child will do. No pressure, but you are one of the most powerful influences in your child's life—perhaps the most powerful. If you want him to thrive, then fully embracing self-care is non-negotiable.

Some parenting needs are practical—help cleaning up the house, a better paying job, more sleep. These needs may feel like failures when you acknowledge them, as if there should be a way for you to handle them more successfully or for you to not need them at all. This self-judgment keeps you stuck. The cycle that emerges goes something like this:

I have unmet needs.

Having needs means I'm not good enough.

I have unmet needs and I'm not good enough.

This thought pattern is not fun, or helpful, or even factually accurate! Even if you're not actively thinking those same words, if similar thoughts brew just below the surface they will erode your self-esteem. Add to that dynamic the daily grind of parenting and you are drained before the alarm clock even rings. This tiresome cycle gets you nowhere. Examining your practical needs is best done by suspending self-judgment and accepting yourself as you are—right here and right now. This may change from day to day. On Saturday morning you may feel well equipped to handle a homework "crisis" or temper tantrum while both of these things may seem impossible to manage at 6:30 p.m. on a Thursday. That's okay. That's the real world. Your internal resources change from hour to hour, and those shifts impact the way you interact with your children and your family. Letting go of self-judgment is a powerful first step toward identifying your needs and working to have them met more consistently.

Other needs are emotional—a desire for partnership and support, the need to give and receive love, wanting to feel appreciated or attractive. These needs are important, and they run deep. In fact, you have probably carried them with you since well before your children showed up, maybe even since you were quite young yourself. Becoming a parent—or a grown-up for that matter—does not magically unpack emotional baggage or ensure fulfillment of your emotional needs. Moreover, if and when you see one of your own emotional needs or vulnerabilities reflected back to you by your child, things can intensify quickly. A parent who struggles with feelings of low self-esteem may be overly sensitive to—or even irritated by—a child who has those same tendencies. A child who possesses strong confidence can also trigger the parent with low self-esteem. A father who had negative experiences playing team sports may be overly hard on his child who shies away from the soccer or baseball field, or may find it hard to embrace a child who is a natural athlete. Basically, your baggage—your unmet emotional needs—often show up in your own child. When they do, you will react with intensity.

It's hard to win, and the best way to move toward resolution is to start by taking care of yourself. Examine your needs truthfully, even if it feels painful at times. Sit with your unmet emotional desires and accept whatever comes up, knowing that the process will allow things to change for the better. The potential gain is tremendous. You just have to be willing to take that initial risk, jump into your emotional basement, and turn the lights on.

Finally, many parental needs involve health. When these go unaddressed, areas of depletion arise and chronic conditions can set in.

Maybe you need to gain control over your blood sugar, or get that mole removed. Are you overdue for a physical, a dental exam, a blood pressure check? Are there things you need to deal with that you just don't seem to have time for—like weight management, pain management, or seeking support for anxiety or depression? Keep in mind that your body may show signs of wear and tear from lack of care or from emotional challenges. Stress takes its toll on the human body right down to the cellular level, so it's no wonder that parents who run on overdrive don't feel so well.

As a parent, if you have had trouble addressing your practical and emotional needs you probably feel like a hamster running on a wheel, living the day just to get into bed again, hoping that somehow things will miraculously change. All the while you may scream your head off and feel crummy about everything. Running on that wheel becomes second nature, and humans are creatures of habit. It will take a conscious effort break this pattern and start meeting your physical needs.

If you need another reminder as to why we're talking about the ways you need to take care of yourself in order to take care of your kids, I'll gladly provide. I work with so many loving, well-intentioned parents who use every tool and strategy I can think of to help improve family functioning—and to no avail. After further discussion, it's common for me

STEPHANIE O'LEARY, PSY.D.   **145**

to learn that the parents are not sleeping adequately, have conditions or deficiencies that are not well managed, or are completely devoid of any personal time for social connections. One mother candidly shared that she was diagnosed as having a severe vitamin D deficiency months prior, but had not yet found time to buy and start taking the supplement recommended to her. She felt completely exhausted and close to falling apart, while tirelessly trying to implement a sleep management plan for her eight-year-old daughter. It was not working because this devoted—yet physically exhausted—mom was falling asleep while tucking her child into bed and thus unable to use any of the strategies we created together.

Don't get me wrong; I am under no illusion that taking a vitamin or getting a check-up is going to lead to children being more compliant and households magically running more smoothly. That's not the case at all. The point is, to help you gain your footing and prepare for the marathon of childrearing—to even have a chance at being in the race—attending to your physical needs must be a top priority. Personally, I have struggled with thyroid issues since my teens. I know that if I do not act quickly when I feel symptoms, my entire family will pay the price because what starts off as a bit of sluggishness quickly devolves into incapacitating fatigue. I have come to value my health and understand that making it a priority serves my children well.

Now it's time to create a game plan, actually a *flight plan*, because the plan involves an oxygen mask and I will serve as your flight attendant—preaching the reminder to tend to yourself before helping others. Grab your computer, your phone's notepad, or a piece of paper and jot down all the things you need. If you're not sure about something, write it down anyway. Go big. No one has to know you have this list so be brutally honest with yourself. This is important and it will help you gain confidence as a parent. Here are some ideas if you're stumped:

POSSIBLE PARENTAL NEEDS

Peace and quiet

Cleanliness and/or order

Exercise and/or movement

Sleep

Love

Nutritious food

Medical care and/or procedures

Haircut

New curtains

Mental health support

Creativity

Strength

Social connections

Prosperity

Laughter

Music

Meditation

Time outdoors or in nature

Affection and/or touch

Fun

The next step is to figure out how to get your needs met in a way that is doable. If you need a peaceful, beautiful place to unwind at the end of the day, a lilac scented candle and some bubble bath is much more likely to happen than a complete bathroom renovation and a new sunken tub. I need peace and quiet but no one in my house has a mute button so I reach for my ear buds and mentally disappear for a ten-minute guided relaxation download. Let's face it, winning the lottery could alleviate a whole bunch of practical needs, but the odds of that coming to fruition are slim to none so you are best served by keeping your plan simple and practical.

Start by picking the top three needs you listed. Jot down three possible ways to meet each of those needs. Don't stress about this; if there is one clear and manageable way to get the job done—great. The important part is to spend time and devote brainpower to your self-care plan while accepting it as a necessary and valuable undertaking.

If this feels hard, pretend you're giving advice to a friend and see how helpful and creative you suddenly become. This strategy will help you access you own best advice without unhelpful critical subtext because it's easier to be kind and understanding to others and hard to resist judgment when you're looking at your own needs in the mirror. Here are some ideas for each category just to help you get your self-care juices flowing:

Possible Needs	Flight Plan to Meet These Needs
Peace and quiet	Download a 10-minute guided meditation and listen each day (possibly while locked in your bathroom or while sitting in your car—alone).
	Carve out alone time. Get a massage, sit in the library, or hang out at a coffee shop. Find your Zen place and go there.
	Take a bath or shower and create a (temporary) sacred space in your bathroom. Make it smell great. Ask and expect not to be interrupted.

Cleanliness and/or order	Identify your pet peeve mess, clean it, and make a family plan so everyone chips in to keep it orderly.
	Create a small space (night table, shelf, etc.) that you commit to keeping free of clutter. Make this space off limits to other family members.
Exercise and/or movement	Devote 20-30 minutes per day to moving in a way that feels good to you. Walk, run, swim, stretch, dance, jump, hike, bike, practice yoga, etc.
	Join an intramural sports team or train for an event (e.g., a 5K).
	Park far away or ditch your car for your bike or feet while traveling locally.
Sleep	Take stock of your bed. Is it comfy? Make changes as needed. Invest in a good pillow.
	Make sure your room is dark and quiet enough. Remove all electronic devices from your nightstand.
	If you have kids in your bed and it's no longer working, create a plan to transition them to their own sleep spaces or create rules regarding the family bed to ensure that you get adequate rest.

Laughter	Listen to comedy.
	Watch your favorite funny movie.
	Surround yourself with people who make you laugh. Make it a priority to be with them.
Love	Be kind and loving to yourself. Keep track of your thoughts. If you find yourself being self-deprecating, acknowledge it and refocus on self-compassion.
	Make time for people and connections that evoke feelings of love and tenderness.
	Journal each day on the ways you love others and the ways you receive love in your life.
Nutritious food	Take stock of your diet. Be honest with yourself. Keep what seems to be working and make one small change a week that you think will help you move toward health.
	Create a family meal plan for the week and ask for help shopping and prepping.
	Buy your favorite nutritious foods and eat slowly so you can savor each bite.

Medical care and/or procedures	Make an appointment with your doctor or health care provider.
	Go to your medical appointments.
	Follow through with medical and lifestyle recommendations or seek a second opinion if you are in doubt.
Beauty	Surround yourself with beautiful, uplifting things, colors, smells, sounds, and textures.
	How do you feel about your physical appearance? If you want to make changes, schedule a haircut, make an appointment for new glasses or contacts, or consult with a skincare specialist.
	When you're getting dressed, think about what makes you feel attractive. If you need to, invest in articles of clothing that make you feel good. Don't overlook the basics like socks and underwear!
Mental health support	Make an appointment with a therapist or counselor and follow through with their recommendations.
	Attend a support group.
	Schedule a physical with your doctor to make sure any underlying medical conditions are identified and addressed.

Meditation	Take a course in meditation.
	Work with a healer or coach to broaden your meditation practice.
	Devote ten minutes a day to practice a guided meditation.
Strength	What are your physical weaknesses? Pick one and do your best to target and strengthen that area for 30 days. After a month, compare your results and see how much you've improved your strength.
	Do as many squats, push-ups, and sit-ups (or whatever exercises you are able to safely do) as you can every day or every other day.
	Journal each day on small ways you observe strength in yourself and others.
Social connections	Take stock of your friendships. Are they healthy and reciprocal? If you find some relationships are out of sync or overwhelming, set boundaries until you feel things are balanced.
	Volunteer for a cause you feel strongly about.
	Send one email or make one call to reconnect with a friend or family member you have not kept in touch with.

Music	Play music you love in the car.
	Listen to your favorite songs while showering.
	Pick up an instrument or practice singing.
Prosperity	Create a change jar. Store all the loose change you and your family generate and cash it in once per month. Use the funds to support your self-care efforts.
	Create a family budget. Be honest. Make changes if necessary.
	Journal each day on how your life is prosperous and include your observations of abundance.
Fun	What makes your heart sing? Make a plan to do it as often as possible.
	Rediscover a hobby or pastime.
	Do something out of the ordinary. Drop your routine and spend time doing something that makes you happy in the moment. Think as big as a responsibly calculated shopping splurge or as small as a sunset stroll before dinner.

Let's review. You've identified some things you need. You've thought about some practical ways to get those needs met. That is definite progress; however, I'm asking you to make a commitment to carrying out your self-care plan because it's easy to lose steam once the real world steps in again and pulls you in ten different directions at once. Plus, you have just shone a spotlight way down into the basement of your life—into all the nooks and crannies that you work hard not to think about or acknowledge. I'm bringing this up because it is a very human response to want to flee from this stuff, these needs. It is easier to pretend you do not have needs because then you can't be held accountable for meeting them. If there's no problem; there's no problem. If there's no need; there's no disappointment. I get it, but that is not genuine. You've turned the lights on and cleaned out your basement of needs. It's hard to prevent old habits and patterns from showing up again, but it's worth it. You have a flight plan and that means you are headed somewhere. You are getting unstuck and taking care of yourself so you can take care of your child.

Before you launch, it's important to quickly review your safety measures. Make sure you know your personal warning bells and emergency alarms. In other words, you have to figure out when you need your oxygen mask because, even after reading this, it still won't drop from the ceiling when you're running on empty (sorry, we tried).

For lots of parents, irritability is one of the first warning signs that a serious self-care break is needed. Losing patience, snapping, and overreacting are all signs that you are depleted and in need of recharging. For some people, physical symptoms may emerge. Anyone prone to joint or back issues, autoimmune struggles, or chronic health conditions knows this. Signs of being down for the count may be a sudden illness that hits you way harder than anyone else in your family, or the sickness that lingers despite your best efforts to kick it. Finally, you may notice negative habits or patterns kick into high gear when unduly stressed. Reaching for something you know is not good for you or avoiding routines that you know help you feel good are surefire signs you need to make time for self-care.

If and when any of these things occur in your household, imagine that each grumble, sniffle, clenched muscle, ache and pain, or strained vocal cord is actually that lovely plastic baggie dandling from the ceiling by a tube. Put on your mask, breathe, and consult your flight plan. Keep copies of your plan handy where you spend most of your time—the kitchen, the car, the office, the notepad of your phone. Follow the steps you outlined to make sure your needs are met because you can't help anyone else if you don't help yourself first.

HOW TO HANDLE OTHER PASSENGERS

Not everyone in your world will have read this chapter. Lots of other parents continue spinning their hamster wheels or simply remain unaware of the concepts you've learned from *Parenting in the Real World*. It's important to talk about this because you are bringing a new idea into practice and it is possible that other people in your life, passengers on your plane so to speak, will not understand or appreciate your plan. It's best to be prepared for this so you are not taken off course.

Consider this: If your son or daughter came home and told you that a kid at school was making fun of them or judging them you would probably have great advice. You would validate them and offer support. Given the opportunity, you might explain that those other kids are probably jealous or dealing with their own challenges and that no one has the right to talk to your child disrespectfully or dismissively. You would encourage your child to keep doing whatever he had been doing that was in line with his needs and ideals, and you would give him your vote of confidence. Your child would come to you saying, "Someone judged me," and you would comfort him and give him permission to continue being himself.

Hold onto that concept and get ready to apply it to yourself as you embark on your self-care plan. Like I said, I want all of your fellow passengers to truly have your best interest at heart. I want to believe that the people in your life are full of good intentions—ready and willing to be supportive and encouraging—but that may not be the case. You may experience turbulence in the form of backlash, grumbles, or even direct judgment for the positive changes you make. If people dish out a sarcastic, "Must be nice!" when you talk about your massage or meditation practice, or your mom or spouse meets you with defensiveness when you ask for help with childcare or chores, you may feel tempted to throw your hands up and go right back to the old way of running yourself ragged.

Please decide right now not to let that happen. Vow to stay on course. All those passengers who have something to say about your priorities or choices are just that—other passengers who feel and think differently than you do. They're not qualified to make the judgments they're dishing out, and even if they were, you're not asking for their opinion, right? You're not seeking permission or validation from those passengers to feel justified in caring for yourself, right? You know that self-care is important, that you cannot possibly be the best mother or father to your child when not meeting your own needs. You know that, right?

Since you know the critical importance of self-care it will be easier to interpret chatter from other passengers as just that: chatter. Meaningless banter that has nothing to do with you or your family's reality. If you can swallow this perspective whole, then any negative feedback you hear may start to become somewhat humorous. You can even treat it like a sitcom or a play with you as the audience member waiting for commentary from the peanut gallery. When it shows up, you can chuckle to yourself and say, "There it is. Meaningless chatter at 2:47 p.m. on Tuesday—check." Expect it, and then see it for what it is. You are more likely to feel judged when you seek approval from others. Side-step this completely by giving yourself permission to take good care of yourself so you can take good care of your kids. They deserve the best, and so do you.

FINAL THOUGHTS ON CHAPTER 7

This self-care stuff may not be the easiest tool to put in your parenting toolbox, but it is one of the most powerful. Be kind and gentle to yourself because you are doing one of the hardest and most important jobs in the world. Get comfortable asking for help. People used to live in villages, and most of us don't anymore. Modern advances have introduced many luxuries into our daily lives, but there are often miles and miles between family members and I truly believe that raising children is not a task best accomplished in isolation. Try to create your own village and accept help when it is offered. You and your children will be the better for it. Even if *stuff* is hitting the fan, at least you will be in good company!

Parenting in the Real World

Takeaways

First, give yourself credit for hanging in until the very end.

Now, to sum up *Parenting in the Real World*, here's your cheat sheet:

- Remember to listen to your child without saying a word. Validate your child so he knows he is heard, and that his thoughts and feelings are worthwhile—even if completely off base.

- Be respectful. Talk to your child the same way you would to a friend or someone in the community. Remember, your child will speak to his or her spouse and children in that very same way down the road.

- Set limits and boundaries so your child learns that limits and boundaries are necessary, and that she can handle them.

- Take full responsibility for your actions. Own your successes and apologize for your mistakes. Remember that saying, "I'm sorry" is overrated. Take responsibility and vow to make a better choice next time.

- Find joy. Fall in love with your child again, and make time and space for laughter and fun.

- Take care of yourself. Meeting your own needs positions you to better meet your child's needs. Do this unapologetically—your kids are counting on you.

Acknowledgements

I want to thank Lisa Tener for her editing skill and encouragement. Tamara Monosoff for her inspiration, enthusiasm, and ongoing support. Annette Giacomazzi for being an amazing person and accountability buddy. Erika Ruggerio for making things beautiful. Alycia Metz for making sure my misuse of commas did not make it to print. Corrine for reading and being excited about what I had to say. Laura for making work fun, for having an amazing sense of humor, and for not thinking I'm crazy (or at least never telling me you think I am). Cathy for believing since a long time ago that I could write this book and for inspiring me not to be afraid.

Mom and Dad for your love, support, and ongoing tolerance of my desire to push the limits.

Steve for technical support and for always making me laugh—although I'm not sure who will have the last laugh if you're ever reading this book for real.

Cindy for always being there no matter how far away you are and for nailing the title!

Quentin for more things than I can write here but mostly for always being in my corner, seeing the best in me, proofreading lots of stuff you probably didn't really want to read, figuring out the page numbers, taking care of the chickens, and making life fun no matter what's going on.

Hannah, thank you for your wardrobe consultations, for teaching me to use Instagram (even though I didn't want to learn), and for being brave enough to share your stories in this book. Owen, thank you for acting as video director, creative assistant, and for starting to make your own lunch even though it's hard to cut the crusts off. I love you both to the stars and back.

And last, but never least, to all the children, parents, and families I have had the honor of working with. Thank you for allowing me to be part of your real world.

Appendix

HOW TO SCAN THE QR CODES IN THIS BOOK

Step 1: Download a free QR code reader onto your smartphone by searching the App Store (I selected the Kaywa Reader because it is free of advertisements).

Step 2: Tap the app once it has downloaded to your phone; this will open up the Reader. Tap again, and your camera will appear to be on. Hover over the code you wish to scan, and the camera will automatically take a picture of the QR code; then your phone will be directed to the web page that contains each video message.

QR CODE A: WALK DOWN MEMORY LANE

As described in Chapter 6, this guided exercise will help you rediscover joy and reconnect with your child by calling to mind all of the endearing qualities and characteristics that make him or her unique and lovable. Starting from the moment you found out you were expecting and ending at the present day, this walk down memory lane will leave you with a renewed appreciation for your child.

http://bit.ly/2dUlJnP

QR CODE B: INTO THE FUTURE

As described in Chapter 6, this guided exercise will help you rediscover joy and reconnect with your child by imagining his or her journey toward the independence of adulthood. This look into the future will give you the perspective and motivation needed to make every moment with your child count as they grow and mature.

http://bit.ly/2eVBf5u

Made in the USA
Middletown, DE
16 November 2018